MANAGING THE JEWISH CLASSROOM

How to Transform Yourself into a Master Teacher

Seymour Rossel

Torah Aura Productions
Los Angeles

To my teachers who are my friends,
to my friends who are my teachers,
and to those rare few who are both—Jacob Behrman,
Manuel Gold, Kenneth Shields, Marshall Terry.

Library of Congress Cataloging-in-Publication #87-040229
International Standard Book Number 0-933873-20-4
©1987 Torah Aura Productions

Torah Aura Productions
4423 Fruitland Avenue
Los Angeles, California, 90058

Manufactured in the United States of America

Table of Contents

UNIT I
A Classroom Management Primer

In this unit

Learning and teaching are two sides of the same coin. Teaching is, by its nature, a profession of self-development. I have been blessed by my colleagues in this respect. Nearly two thousand teachers have participated in my workshops over the past fifteen years. And I have managed to learn much from them. One thing I learned is that teachers respect and value most those techniques which they can immediately translate into action. I incorporate this valuable piece of learning into every workshop I plan. Today my teacher workshops are made up entirely of things teachers can use the very next time they stand before a class. In this first unit you will find a distillation of basic techniques: how to get the most out of this book, how to keep from going stale, how to keep a lesson from bogging down, how to insure that students are motivated, how to head off discipline problems, and how to set the proper atmosphere for learning. And , because it is of primary significance, you will also find a brief chapter on the meaning of Jewish education.

Chapter 1
How to use this book to gain a personal teaching style.

In this chapter

This is a book about teaching and learning. It could be used by any teacher. But it is designed specifically for the Jewish teacher. The inherent philosophy is Jewish. And the examples throughout are drawn from Jewish contexts. In writing this book, I have used several simple rules to guide me. You have already encountered Rule #1, the same rule which I apply to my workshops: If a technique or idea cannot be used by teachers the very next time they stand before a class, it is not included.

If you wish, you can skip this chapter and go directly to Chapter 2. In Chapter 2, I deal only with things that will be useful in your classroom. But you might be interested in the other rules which I used as I was writing; and I believe that knowing them can help you get the most out of using this book.

Rule #2—**brevity**. If I can abbreviate a thing clearly, I do so. Teachers have a tendency to become pedantic (a rather nice word for "long-winded"). Readers—and students—seem to prefer to receive material at a quickened pace rather than bearing with lengthy verbiage. As an avid reader, I could not agree more.

Rule #3—**repetition**. If something is important enough, it bears repetition. Even after a subject has been mastered, review keeps it alive and vibrant. In language learning, for example, no matter how fluent the student of a language becomes, a lack of opportunity to use and review the language and its rules causes that knowledge to wither and, eventually, to die. Of course, even in repetition, I obey Rule

A study of textbooks done in the '70s observed that any material presented as "caption" text—notes accompanying a drawing or illustration, main and subheads, boxed text, and marginal material—stands a better than average chance of being read. In other words, the percentages say you will read these marginal notes. If you do, here's what you will find: 1. some of my favorite quotations, 2. ideas that somehow did not quite fit the flow of the text, 3. stray observations or anecdotes, and 4. a challenge or two that has sparked an idea for me and that might spark an idea for you. (Most citations are given in full in the bibliography.)

All over the world people are spending their lives either doing jobs where the mind must be kept numb all day, or on highly-rewarded activities which are tedious or frivolous. One can get accustomed to operating an adding-machine for five and a half days a week, or to writing advertisements to persuade the public that one brand of cigarettes is better than another. Yet no one would do either of these things for its own sake. Only the money makes them tolerable. But if you really understand [and study] important and interesting subject[s]...it is a genuine happiness to explain them to others, to feel your mind grappling with their difficulties, to welcome every new book on them, and to learn as you teach.
—Gilbert Highet, *The Art of Teaching*.

#2—brevity. (Notice how I used repetition and brevity in one and the same sentence? That leads me to Rule #4.)

Rule #4—**replication**. No technique is worth studying if a teacher cannot easily replicate it in the classroom. In schools of education students spend innumerable hours devouring hierarchies and taxonomies. When they actually face students, they suddenly discover that human beings are not easily pigeon-holed into categories. Human beings are too complex for facile classifications. When I describe a hierarchy or a taxonomy, I turn it into a model for usage. If it cannot be modeled for usage, it does not belong in this book. (It would not make it into one of my workshops, either.)

Rule #5—**simplicity of terminology**. I will describe many teaching models. Some of these models were developed by great teachers and deduced by great researchers. Some were developed by teachers, students, and researchers who have taken part in my classes and workshops. The former usually come replete with a great deal of "intellectualese"—language intended to render them scholarly or erudite. I believe we can, for the most part, dispense with that language. The ideas are important, not the proprietary terms used to introduce them. Babies are often born with a great deal of hair, known as *vellus* hair. Most of this early growth disappears soon after birth, to be replaced later by a healthy growth of normal (what scientists call "terminal") hair. In presenting ideas and models, I have opted to present terminal hair rather than newborn decoration.

These are my simple rules.

1. Ideas must be practical.
2. They must be presented briefly and clearly.
3. They must be periodically reviewed and reiterated for emphasis.
4. They must be replicable in any classroom.
5. They must be presented in ordinary terms to make them accessible.

In line with these rules, I have a few suggestions for you, the reader. Whether you are a veteran or a new recruit, I believe that following these few guidelines can be extremely helpful to you.

First, approach this book as you would a laboratory course. As you read each chapter, experiment with the ideas and techniques in your classroom. Like any trial runs, some of these will immediately work, while others will require some personalization or modification. Keep experimenting with a technique until you have mastered it and made it your own. Second, use the book like a tutorial. Don't try to master it all at once. Read a chapter, try out one or two new things in your classroom, then come back for another chapter. If you do read the book cover to cover, go back and reread it a chapter at a time. This will probably be the best way to absorb the material.

Third, make notes. The best way to know when real learning has taken place is to ask a student to rephrase the learning in his or her own words. Making notes is the closest I can come to this dialogue in a book (by their nature, books tend to be monologues). If you make notes, you will know whether something is completely clear or if it is still elusive. You will recognize what you need to look at again. And you will realize when you have learned something new, or recalled something useful that you already knew.

Fourth, don't store your memory on paper. Many students take copious notes and forget to learn anything. They are merely storing memory on paper. They believe that they will go back and refer to these notes. But the truth of the matter is that they use notebook upon notebook to fill bookshelves and filing cabinets (and drawers and desk-tops). If something seems really useful, commit it to memory. (Memorization is a Jewish tradition. For hundreds of years at a time, Jewish knowledge was passed from generation to generation by mastery and memorization.) To help you in memorizing important ideas, I present them in threes, fours, and fives, and sometimes in tens. You will be surprised, I think, how easily these groupings penetrate and and how long they remain firmly implanted once they are memorized.

Fifth, if memorizing seems daunting, don't bother doing it consciously. Trust your unconscious. Neuropsychologists tell us that our unconscious minds work twenty-four hours a day. We unconsciously record everything we read, everything we do, everything said to us, and everything we say, see, and feel. For some people, getting the "feel" of this book will be more important than reading every word. For others, seeing the techniques in tabular or graphic form will be more important than the verbiage. Still others will hang on every word. No matter which of these is your preference, you will be pleasantly surprised if you trust your unconscious as much as your conscious. When an appropriate situation arises, you will see the right technique, or recall reading the right method, or feel yourself handling the situation as the book intended. You can rely on that, even when you feel

One must learn
By doing the thing; for
though you
Think you know it
You have no certainty,
until you try.
—Sophocles, *Trachiniae*

Every day I learn so much. I hope the children are learning some, too, but they couldn't possibly learn more than a fraction of what I have. I think there is hope for me yet.
—Jean Morris, "Diary of a Beginning Teacher," *NASSP Bulletin* 52 (October 1968).

The best ideas are common property.
—Seneca, *The Epistles.*

that you cannot rely on your ability to memorize. (Actually, you will be relying on both these innate talents, and, in time, you may learn to trust them both, too.)

Last, always remember that what I am saying is true *for me*—it is not necessarily true for you. You have to make it true for you. The secret of transforming yourself into a master teacher is that *you* must transform *yourself*. No one can do this for you.

A group of ḥasidim once came to study with their rebbe and found him sitting and weeping. They tried to console him.

"Why are you crying?" they asked.

"When I was a young man," he said, "I thought I could change the world, so I set out to try. That's how I learned that the world is a very difficult thing to change.

"When I turned thirty, I decided that it was just as important for me to perfect my small corner of the world, so I placed all my energies in trying to improve my community and my students.

"That's how I learned that communities and classes cannot be made perfect.

"So, at the age of forty, I set about to change just my family. I spent hours and hours with my wife and my children, trying to make my family perfect. But I learned that even families cannot be perfected.

"When I reached my maturity, I realized that there was only one who would listen to the lessons I had been placed in the world to teach, so I set out to perfect myself. But now I know that even that is beyond my powers."

The students were afraid. If the rebbe could not perfect himself, what chance had they? They turned to consoling him even more. "Rebbe, you have become a *tzaddik*—what you do is right and just. You should not cry because you are not perfect. Only God can be perfect."

"No," said the rebbe, "you misunderstand. I am not weeping because I am sad. I am weeping because of the great blessing which God has granted me."

"What blessing?" the students demanded.

"All through my life," the rebbe answered, "God has given me the strength to try."

Some say that what was really given at Mount Sinai was style.
—Ḥayyim N. Bialik

Chapter 2
Remaining Relevant

In this chapter

Capturing the students' attention is essential. Even the work of motivation cannot begin if the student and teacher are not on the same wavelength. And the transformation of teaching into learning depends on teachers, students, and parents working cooperatively. This chapter contains a series of simple and tested activities which help teachers, students, and parents interact in useful ways.

Like most things, remaining relevant seems deceptively easy when successful. Master teachers approach relevance with inimitable style. Yet, when examined closely, their techniques reveal a pattern which can easily be replicated. For practicality, I have divided them into things which can be done at the beginning of the class year, things which should be done throughout the class year, and things which are most effective at the end of the year.

FIRST DAY AND EARLY IN THE YEAR
Taking Inventory

The self-inventory is one of many activities developed by the values clarification movement. This model can be used by any teacher to gain a working inventory of individual student interests.

Give each student a large index card. Draw the outline of a card on the chalkboard. Number from 1 to 6 along the left hand side of the outline card on the chalkboard, and ask students to do the same on their individual cards. As you call for various items, indicate on the chalkboard the relative placement of the items and give a brief general description (a single word, if possible).

In the upper left corner, ask students to print their

While you are taking inventories, consider taking a self-inventory. This is generally a more difficult process. Inside, your psychological barriers are sturdily built and well defended. You will need to break them down a bit to learn more about who you really are.

Here's a simple way: Imagine a newspaper devoted exclusively to reporting you. You are its star reporter. Give it a masthead and motto. Write your news of the day. Add the features—sports, drama, society news, comics, cooking, art, travel, letters to the editor, and so on. Then, add classifieds and advertisements (touting you, of course). Do this in writing or on a typewriter, or even on a large sheet of oak tag. Set it aside for a day or two. Then, come back to it as if you were the City Editor. Be hypercritical about everything. Is it truthful? Is it believable? Does it answer who, what, when, where, why, and how? If not, fix it. Set it aside again. When you come back, be the subscriber. Read it.

If this works for you, try doing a family newspaper with your immediate family. Let each family member choose the areas most interesting to him or her personally.

Getting to know others will be more valuable if it's part of the larger process of getting to know how others fit into the world you have made for yourself.

names (note: you may vary any placements to suit your own taste).

In the upper right corner , you may wish to ask students for class name and room number (especially if you are teaching more than one class simultaneously).

Ask for the following 6 items:

1. A book read recently (or over the summer). Ask students to list a book they themselves chose, or one presently in their room at home. If they have not recently read a book, ask them to fill in the name of a book they read and enjoyed in the past.
2. A favorite recent movie.
3. A favorite music group or song.
4. A favorite hobby or interest.
5. A favorite television series.
6. A brief sentence telling what they would most like to learn in your class this year.

Please note: Teachers of young children must modify this technique slightly. Provide a large manila sheet with the child's name and the numbers already recorded. Instead of words, use pictures. For each category, teacher and class should develop a short list of possible answer. Discuss choices aloud with the class. Ask students to draw an "X" for choice A, an "O" for choice B, a "+" for choice C, and so on. By keeping a record of the choices, the teacher can easily tabulate the results.

Collect the index cards. It is not necessary to discuss them in class. These index cards, when arranged and tabulated, can provide you with many valuable insights regarding the students in your classroom. They provide a picture of the students' world—what students on their own choose to see, hear, and feel. To properly utilize this material, you will have to listen to some of the popular recordings or recording groups, watch some the most popular television series, see the most popular movies, and read the most popular books.

You are likely to find that children, like their elders, have a "hit parade" of favorites. By reading only a few principal books, seeing only a few principal movies, and learning a few facts about a few principal recording stars or movie stars, you will be ready to use many references to these "student favorites" in your teaching. Young people like to know that their teachers are not isolated from the "realities." And, since each student individually assigns meaning to "reality"—defining it in terms of what he or she knows and experiences—when a teacher shows recognition and appreciation for the student's "reality" the implication is that the teacher recognizes and appreciates the student.

Tapping Parent Resources

Parents have great influence on their children. What parents think and say about the classroom and the teacher has a direct and immediate impact on the child and, by extension, the class. At the same time, parents have well-developed and complex personalities. In addition to their personal histories, educational backgrounds, and professions, they typically engage in sports, hobbies, travel, and other pursuits. Most parents sincerely try to provide good role models for their children to follow. Most earnestly wish for school classes to succeed. Thus, they can be a valuable resource for enriching educational experiences.

Early in the school year, Send home a "parent inventory" sheet, asking parents to fill out and return it. Make it possible for parents to give brief answers to the questions. (This enhances the chances that forms will be completed and returned.) Ask parents to list hobbies, travel, interests, high school or college majors, professions, etc. Ask if they would be willing to come into class one or more times to share experience or expertise. Collect the forms. Tabulate forms by talents, skills, etc.

Please note: If possible, create two forms—one for single-parent families and one for "mom and pop" operations. Make sure each student gets a form appropriate for his or her family. This extra touch of consideration may go unnoticed. On the other hand, using a general form requiring answers from both a mother and a father may be perceived as insensitivity on the part of the teacher or school, and may even, in some cases, cause friction between parent and child.

When teaching teenagers, be sure to check first with the teenager before inviting a parent to the classroom. Some teenagers are embarrassed by watching their parents "perform" for their friends. Use your own sensitivity to judge when it is and when it is not appropriate to include parents of teenagers in your teaching plans.

As you map out units for the year, consider how parents might contribute to the lessons. Call on parents. Discuss and plan with them. Allot them small segments of class time (many parents will consider ten to fifteen minutes of engaged time more than enough teaching).

In class, parents can be interviewed, included in round-table discussions, asked to describe interesting life experiences, assigned actual teaching roles, given moderator roles for small-group work, etc. Choices for utilizing parents effectively in the classroom should be governed by your subject, their level of expertise, their perception of their own teaching abilities, and your perception of their teaching abilities.

Please note: This technique, with slight modification, is also effective when teaching adults. Ask adults with applicable experiences and backgrounds to prepare to teach parts of lessons.

THROUGHOUT THE YEAR
Checking environmental changes

Spend a few minutes before class—and during breaks between subject segments, during recess or lunch, and at other odd moments—chatting with students. Ask about books they are reading, new movies, new television shows, hobbies, travel, fads, fashions, and other phenomena. Try to recall and note some of these responses on the student "inventory" index cards. Follow through by learning more about new parts of the student's environment, and refer to them in your teaching, when appropriate.

Maintaining Parental Contact

Contact parents well before the first grading period, and continue regular contact throughout the year. Especially useful are a few of the following techniques:

A **Newsletter** including materials authored by the class and your own "editorial."

Homework designed to be done jointly by either parent (see the note above regarding single parent families) and the student.

Notes sent home regarding the beginning and end of units of instruction.

Parent reading lists related to the subjects being studied by the class.

Random telephone calls to parents to check on how they perceive that their child's year is progressing (and how they perceive that their child is progressing, too). Try to make a

I BELIEVE THAT
The school is primarily a social institution. Education being a social process, the school is simply that form of community life in which all those agencies are concentrated that will be most effective in bringing the child to share in the inherited resources of the race, and to use his own powers for social ends.

Education, therefore, is a process of living and not a preparation for future living.
—John Dewey, *My Pedagogic Creed*, 1897.

few calls each week. On a list, check off parents you have contacted and try to contact all parents at least once each semester.

Maintaining student contacts

From time to time, try to contact students outside normal school hours. This encourages students to become more personally involved with you, sometimes helps to alleviate aberrant classroom behaviors, and, in general, establishes a more solid rapport. A personal letter in the mailbox or, if you prefer, a personal phone call, might address a special assignment or just chat about classwork and indicate how the student is doing. If you do this, try to be methodical:

Check off students who have received personal communications.

Contact all students at least once each semester.

Please note: Students sometimes indicate a desire to enter into ongoing correspondence. Feel free to engage in and even enjoy this correspondence, but try to keep your goal in mind. If a student stops writing, don't let yourself feel hurt or abandoned. Students have many time commitments, and often feel overwhelmed. Despite their best intentions—even promises—they sometimes allow their correspondence to trickle off. If you react in an offended, hurt, or punitive fashion, you will defeat the purpose of the correspondence. Let defaults pass, and the good effects of communication already accomplished will generally remain.

The "Positive Report Card"

One very powerful technique brings the teacher into the student's world with the help of the parent or parents. The positive report card gets its special power from the fact that it creates a bond which automatically enhances the teacher's relevance to the world of the student.

From a local post office, purchase a handful of pre-stamped postcards. Keep them handy in your desk or attached with a rubber band to a notebook or roll book.

When a student performs well in a given subject area on a given occasion, or when a student behaves in a particularly positive manner on a given occasion, make an immediate mental note (or, if necessary, jot down the name of the student then and there, along with a word or two to help you recall the specifics of the positive incident later).

Being Positive

Here are some rules for positive classroom reinforcement:

1. In teaching a new task, reinforce immediately rather than permit a delay between response and reinforcement.

2. In the early stages of a task, reinforce every correct response. As learning occurs, require more correct responses prior to reinforcement; gradually shift to intermittent reinforcement.

3. Reinforce improvements or steps in the right direction. Do not insist on perfect performance on the first try.

4. Don't reinforce undesirable behavior.

—based on studies conducted by B. F. Skinner as summarized in Myron H. Dembo, *Teaching for Learning*.

At the end of the day, or during a break, take a moment to address a card to the parent or parents of the outstanding student. On the back of the postcard, briefly communicate that this is just a note to "commend" so-and-so and "inform" the family that so-and-so was outstanding in class today. Be sure to include enough detail so that the student, when questioned by the parent, will be able to reconstruct what it was that made the teacher so happy.

There are several "essentials" in this technique. It is essential that the post card be directed to the parent or parents, rather than the child. Your goal is to create an opportunity for parent, teacher, and student to share in enjoyment.

It is equally essential that the postcard be sent in the mail—and that it be mailed the same day or the very next day. The effect of receiving the card in the mail can be astounding. If it comes soon enough, student and parent will join in discussion not only about the specific incident, but about the class in general.

It is also essential to use the pre-stamped postcards available from the postal service. After observing many teachers using this technique over many years, I can vouch for this: Those who tried to improve it by using picture postcards or memo forms or other media invariably delayed mailing the report as they searched for appropriate postage stamps or the correct-sized envelope. Delays of a day or two can be critical in this technique, and tend to take the edge off the good that positive report cards can do.

Positive Report Cards help make the class seem relevant to the student and extend the influence of the teacher into the home where it is matched by the approbation of the parent. And what parents consider most relevant, children tend to consider most relevant.

The Positive Report Card: A Case Study

Consider, for example, the case of the typical student involved in aberrant classroom behavior. His or her parents grow accustomed to hearing from the school only in conjunction with behavior problems This, in turn, grows into a wish that they would hear no more from the school. (This is really a wish that the child would change behavior patterns so that the school would no longer be forced to call.) Suddenly, a postcard comes from you, the teacher, and, to the utter astonishment of everyone—student, parent, siblings— it is about a moment (even an instant, depending on the child's usual classroom behavior) in which the tables turned (even if only by accident). For the first time in a long time, perhaps, the parent can see a glimmer of a new possible future for the child in school. The family can share a positive moment, reinforcing what went on as "commendable" or "model" behavior. A smile, a pat on the head, a hug, a handshake, or some other expressive action on the part of the parent may well ensue, as well as the question, "Why can't you be that way more often?" Such positive reinforcement from the family—the unit in which most of the student's world is invested—may even lead the student to wonder, "Why shouldn't I do this more often?"

The result may not be immediate, despite the immediate positive reward. In tough cases, it may take more than one positive report, and several other forms of personal contact and demonstrations of teacher concern. But this technique can result in a breakthrough, a beachhead from which the artillery can begin its assault on problem behavior. And, just as this is true of the student who is a discipline problem, it is also true of every student. Too often, parents hear only about final judgments—at report periods or teacher conferences—without being able to share the experience of, and reward the child for, the everyday satisfactions of the classroom.

The Positive Report Card thus serves many functions—asserting the relevance of the teacher within the family circle, giving opportunities for positive reinforcement within the all-encompassing home environment, conveying opportunities for parents and children to share information about the classroom, and even opening a breach within which the changing of behavior becomes a realistic and achievable goal. All this for a very minimal investment of time!

It is important to note, however, that in the case of junior high and older students this strategy becomes less effective as the teenager becomes more heavily invested in the peer group and less so in the family unit.

AT THE CLOSE OF THE YEAR
Feeding-forward

At the close of a semester or a year, there are few obligations placed on the teacher with regard to the student directly. And there is generally a lack of follow-through. But what happens just after an action can be important to the action's goal. Follow-through is as essential in good teaching as it is in good tennis.

Teachers rarely get feedback from past students, but there are ways to insure that the relevance of what was taught may continue to reverberate in the student's life after the course is ended. I refer to these techniques as "feeding-forward."

It is not enough for students to learn a subject, they must also become consciously aware of having learned. The student must feel that the teacher has imparted something important. In later years, will students remember what was gained in a particular classroom, under the tutelage of a particular teacher? Inevitably, the answer is that some will and some will not. The following are a few ways of weighting the odds in your favor.

The Memory Book

One way to insure feed-forward is to provide a summary in written form. This technique draws on the old idea of a "class autograph party" on the last day of school.

For the last day of your class, ask students to bring inexpensive looseleaf binders and five or six pages of

Most people, as we see, stop growing between thirty and forty. They "settle down"—a phrase which implies stagnation—or at the utmost they "coast along," using their acquired momentum, applying no more energy, and gradually slowing down to a stop. No teacher should dream of doing this. His job is understanding a large and important area of the world's activity and achievement and making it viable for [his students]. He should expect to understand more and more of it as the years go by.
—Gilbert Highet, *The Art of Teaching.*

notebook paper. Be sure to have a few binders filled with paper on hand for forgetful students.

Ask the students to label the covers of their notebooks with their names, class and teacher; label the first page "Memories;" and label each of the subsequent pages, "Classmates."

Lead a class discussion on what was taught during the year. Write the best summaries, or the most salient points, on the chalkboard. When you have five or six prime examples, ask the students to copy these on the first page of their notebooks. Ask each student to add one more of his/her own most important memories.

Allow students to circulate with their notebooks, to exchange signatures and comments with one another. (You may also wish to remind them to exchange addresses and telephone numbers.) You, as the teacher, can also participate in this exchange, especially to be sure that everyone has a few "friends" to record.

Send the memory book home with the students. Its benefits will linger on.

Class Trivia

There is still another way to close the class with a feeling of camaraderie. During the year, make notes of interesting, amusing, and awkward class moments. Toward the end of the year, write these up, and make a handout for the students. Ask them to add their own memories, either verbally or in writing. Make sure to include some of the highlights of the subject matter, as well—interesting lessons, lesson plans that worked especially well, humorous and practical test questions, etc. Be sure to praise and thank the class for being able to work together closely throughout the year. Wish them a good summer, and suggest to them that the next year can be just as enjoyable as this one was.

This technique can be effective even in cases where the year was not particularly good for the class, or in the case of a particularly difficult class. It lays the groundwork for a change over the summer, and may be very helpful to the next teacher.

The Sneak Preview

Last, but not least, you may wish to provide a sneak preview of what's next. Students like to feel they are progressing and growing. Telling them how this year's curriculum relates to next year's can give them a real sense of this growth, reaffirm just how relevant your class and subject have been, and reflect well on your own concern for them—all at once.

Prepare a short handout giving the main topics of the next year's curriculum. Distribute this sheet on the last day of class. Ask students to discuss how this year has helped to prepare them for next year. Ask students to place a star beside the topics for next year that they think will be most interesting to them, then a dot beside those which they think will be most important to their future lives.

All of these techniques share a commonality in that they all require an awareness of the world as students perceive it. At the same time, all of them are simple to accomplish.

In sum, retaining your relevance as a teacher means understanding the students' subjective reality. This reality—like all realities—is made up of the things which affect your students in a personal way. To the extent that you become familiar with these things, you include yourself in the student's "circle" of awareness. In other words, you are "relevant." And this relevance will extend itself to your subject matter, as well. The more interested and concerned you are, the more interesting your subject matter becomes *ipso facto*. The more you seem to enjoy what your students enjoy, the more easily you will be able to gain their respect and their cooperation. The object is not to become one of them, not to be a "friend" in the narrow sense of a "peer", but rather to be a "friend" in the larger sense—a mentor, a companion willing to point out a new trail and walk with them for a way. A good travel guide is always relevant.

Chapter 3
"If You Don't Know Where You Are Going, Any Road Will Get You There"

In this chapter

Great teachers are great communicators. In the words of the last chapter, they are travel guides. Everyone is called upon to give directions, but only the best teachers turn direction-giving into an art form. This chapter contains a simple, four-step model that can save you valuable class time.

As a Jewish sage once warned, "If you don't know where you are going, any road will get you there." This is good advice, but overly optimistic. Things are much worse. Some roads go directly to nowhere.

Among many possible variables in good teaching, *The Beginning Teacher Study** chose to include a measurement of "transition time," the time spent moving from one activity or lesson part to another. Transition time may be spent in clean-up, as at the close of an arts and crafts project, in giving directions for what is coming next, in movement from one part of the classroom to another, or in a hundred similar ways.

Transition time quickly adds up. In one particular class in which the school day consisted of 300 minutes, researchers identified a full 76 minutes of transition time! And this was the classroom of a "creative" teacher! This teacher set up a listening center, a silent reading table, a math facts table, a career education table, a science center, a cooking station, and more in the classroom. Students moved in and out of the various centers rapidly throughout the day. Trying to be creative, this teacher was actually losing one quarter of the available instructional time each day to commuting.

The Beginning Teacher Evaluation Study, reported in 1978, dealt with teaching factors that directly impact learning. Because it was a statistical study, conclusions must be tempered with the understanding that statistics can be bent to fit theories—and often are. The debate as to whether education is best studied by statistical or qualitative measurement rages fiercely. Following Maimonides' principle of judgment, the truth probably lies in neither camp, except that both types of study, taken in context, provide valuable insights.

*Fisher and others. *Teaching Behaviors, Academic Learning Time and Student Achievement.* San Francisco, CA: Far West Laboratory, 1978.

Time wasted in ineffective direction-giving, or time wasted in large numbers of transitions cannot be replaced. Creativity must be balanced against time constraints. This is especially true in the Jewish school, where our time is extremely limited. Jewish teachers must make every moment count.

Planning for clarity

If you were giving a stranger directions to get to your house, you might a) draw a map, b) write out the directions in words, c) define well-known landmarks, or d) offer your telephone number in case the directions were insufficient.

To be sure that the stranger understood the directions, you might a) ask the stranger to repeat them verbatim, b) watch the stranger as he or she took the directions to see if his or her head was nodding affirmatively or shaking negatively, or c) ask the stranger to repeat the directions in his or her own words.

One thing is certain: You would never ask the stranger to go to your house first, then get the directions for getting there!

On the surface that seems obvious, but in practice, teachers often do just this. They may begin with something like: "Get into groups of five," then wait until the noise settles down and the students are divided into small clusters before telling the students what the clusters should do. Automatically, transition time doubles, as the teacher has to reclaim the students' attention before giving the directions.

Other teachers rely heavily on the students' memories. They may begin with something like: "Get into groups of five. Choose a recorder and a moderator. Discuss how you would change the first sentence of the third paragraph on page 118. Write down one answer for the group," and so on. They often find themselves repeating the same instructions several times.

Step #1 for giving directions is **plan for clarity**. For any activity you present in the classroom, make sure you have a clear list of the exact instructions before you start.

Use Examples

Step #2 is **use examples**. An extra minute or two to provide a precise working example will save many minutes of wasted effort on the part of the students and the teacher.

Which of these two sets of directions would you rather follow?

DIRECTION SET A

"In a minute, we are going to divide into groups of five. I will give each group of five a paper bag containing three objects. Your bag might have in it a rubber band, a clipboard, and a handkerchief. Your job is to create a religion that uses all three of these things. For example, you could call your religion 'hospitalism.' The high priest could wear the handkerchief over her nose and mouth to keep germs from flying as she prays to the 'hospital god.' The rubber band could be used to attach a name bracelet around the wrist of a worshiper to show that he is a "patient-member" of the religion. The clipboard could be used to hold pieces of paper with strange writing on them— this could be the priest's 'chart of religious progress.' When you have decided what the name of your religion is, and how the three things are going to be used, let me know by raising your hands. In ten minutes, or when all the groups are finished—whichever comes first—we will share our new 'religions' with one another."

DIRECTION SET B

"In a minute we will divide into groups of five. I will give each group of five a paper bag containing three objects. Your job is to 'create' a religion that uses all three of these things. When you have decided what the name of your religion is, and how the three things are going to be used, let me know by raising your hands. Then we will share our new 'religions' with one another."

Just reading this, you can tell at once that direction set A is going to produce richer results. Examples help students know exactly what is expected of them. Even if your planned activity is something "original," like a poem or drawing, examples can help. Students need to know how long the poem should be, how much detail to include in the drawing. The clearer the goal, the more explicit the example, the better the result.

Using the chalkboard

Step #3 is, if you can **make it visual**, do!

If you are planning to divide the class into four groups, and you want the groups in the four corners of the classroom—not randomly pressing against one another—draw a square on the chalkboard; label it "room"; put a circle in each corner of the square; label the circles "group 1," "group 2," and so on; and say, "This is how I want you to arrange your chairs when we break into groups."

If you are good at drawing flow charts, you can put an abbreviated set of directions on the chalkboard in the form of a flow chart.

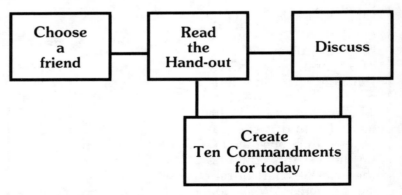

If you are not comfortable with such visual representations, you can list abbreviated directions for the activity on the chalkboard, as you explain the directions verbally.

Teacher:	*Chalkboard:*
"First divide into groups of three."	1. Find two friends.
"Choose a commandment from the list of ten commandments I give you."	2. Choose 1 commandment.
"Together with your group, find one reason that this is a good commandment."	3. Reason it's good.
"Together with your group, explain one situation in which following the commandment might be a bad thing to do."	4. When it may be bad.

Some teachers prefer to write directions on the chalkboard before giving them to the students verbally. Then, as you give each step in the directions, point with finger or chalk to that direction on the chalkboard.

All of these techniques will ultimately save you a great deal of transition time. Pictures—even word pictures—can make directions much easier to follow.

Reiteration

Teacher studies show that a real proof of learning is when Step #4: **students are able to repeat what the teacher has said in their own words**. When we speak of techniques for making learning memorable, we will have much more to say about this. But it is true of directions as well.

One way to be sure that directions are clear is to watch the students as the directions are being given. If a student shakes his or her head from side to side, or looks quizzically at the chart or list of directions, then stop and say something like, "Zeke, do you have a question about this?" If several class members display this kind of behavior, repeat the directions a second time, using a second set of examples. If the behavior persists, you should stop and ask for any questions the students might have.

Even if everyone nods affirmatively, you may wish to ask someone in the class to repeat the directions. If students cannot reiterate (repeat the material in their own words), go back and start over. A little extra time on directions makes for a better chance of success for an assignment.

Giving directions clearly is sometimes complex. And hearing things in the way students hear them can be something of an art. That is why reiteration—the students' rephrasing of the directions given—is essential. At least, this repetition is a way of telling what is going wrong.

For example, consider the story of the teacher who placed her hand on her chest and said, "This is where the heart is." One of the students immediately opined, "Mine is where I sit!"

The teacher asked, "What gives you that idea?" to which the student replied, "Whenever I do something nice, my grandma pats me on the bottom and says, 'Bless your little heart.'"

Before schooling became compulsory—in the halcyon days when education was considered an advantage to be sought—homework was done willingly. These days are past. As Gilbert Highet once remarked, "Scarcely anybody learns the multiplication-table for fun." That sage of education, Michel Eyquem de Montaigne, suggested that those who refused to learn or were incapable of learning should be strangled "if there are no witnesses, or else should be apprenticed to a pastry-cook in some good town." Since we do not have the luxury of the one nor the tendency toward the other (you may guess the assignments of these referents) the next most practical thing is to give homework assignments which are brief and fun to accomplish. More on that, below.

Homework— the last word on direction-giving

If the directions are for homework, the rules—one to four—become doubly important. You can't be at home with each student to answer questions or dispel doubts about the homework. Therefore, homework assignments with a succinct example—or two, in the case of difficult assignments—should ideally be typed out clearly on a paper and given to each student. They should be carefully reviewed in class, using the piece of paper like a chalkboard—or putting the steps on the chalkboard itself. And you should be sure that every member of the class understands and can reiterate the assignment. Last, but not least, all of this must be done before the bell rings ending the school day or the teaching hour.

A Thumbnail Review

In brief then, this is the four-step model:
1. Plan for clarity—be certain you know the steps and can clearly explain them to the class.
2. Use examples—paint a picture of how the activity or exercise can be successfully completed.
3. If you can make it visual, do!—use the chalkboard effectively in direction-giving.
4. Call for reiteration—ask student(s) to repeat the directions as understood, not as given.

   If you follow this model, you will find that transition time will shrink, and the quality of the completed work will rise.

Chapter 5

Motivation 101: Success in Introducing Subject Matter

In this chapter

Much educational research has been done in the area of motivation—helping students to prepare to learn. This chapter cites some basic work on human needs and explores ways teachers can use the many levels of needs which all human beings share. Three needs which are specific to learning (and which are really motivational needs) are spelled out in some detail. Last, a technique for tapping into these needs—set induction—is discussed, with some practical examples of how it can be used.

The Keys to Motivation
The Basic Needs

In an article in *Psychological Review* (1943, Vol. 50, 370-396), Abraham H. Maslow defined the basic needs of all individuals. "Needs" are driving forces that tend to dominate the individual. These forces range from very primitive to very sophisticated. As each level of needs is met, new and more subtle needs arise which become dominant. Individuals are never "satisfied," we always have needs of some kind.

First, Maslow lists the physiological needs—water content of the blood, salt content, sugar content, protein content, fat content, calcium content, oxygen content, hydrogen-ion level (acid-base balance) content, and constant temperature. These needs lead to *homeostasis*—keeping the body on an even keel. If these and similar bodily needs are met, needs for safety arise.

Needs for safety include a desire for a caring environment (usually, the family), for human society to protect us from wild animals, and for protection from extremes of temperature, criminals, assault and murder, tyranny, and so on. If these needs are satisfied, other needs arise—for example, the need for love.

Love needs include the desire for warmth and friendship from other human beings—first from sweethearts or family, then from neighbors and significant others. Maladjustment in society often stems from the thwarting of love needs. But, once love is assured, it is superseded by needs for esteem.

People generally wish to have a sense of self-worth, and a reasonably high evaluation of themselves. Needs for esteem include the desire for strength, achievement, adequacy, confidence in the world, independence and freedom. If these needs are met, they are supplanted by needs for self-actualization.

Whenever a threat occurs to any basic need, the individual immediately reverts to the level of that need and does everything necessary or possible to try to satisfy it.

How These Needs Impinge on the Classroom

That is theory. Let's examine a practical example of how Maslow's investigation of human needs might affect the classroom.

Teacher X is rolling along with a nice lesson plan. By and large, the students are following the discussion and the teacher is employing an interactive question-and-answer dialogue. When one student answers, however, the answer is so far out of context that Teacher X says to the student, "That's the worst answer a student ever gave," or "A turkey could give a better answer than that!"

The student feels attacked. Confronted with this kind of teacher response, the student reverts to a lower level on the needs scale. Learning needs are set aside. Self-actualization needs are set aside. Love needs have been attacked. The student must now find some way of recovering a sense of warmth and friendship from the teacher. Since that is difficult in a class setting, the student is more likely to seek peer approval. And an easy way to obtain peer approval in the classroom is through "acting out"—behavior which undermines the teacher. A teacher response which personally attacks a student, then, is an invitation to the student to misbehave.

This is even more obvious (and works even more to the detriment of the teacher) when it is not just a love need which is assailed, but a safety need. "If I catch you passing notes again, I will call your parents," is a threat which produces an instinctive reversion to safety needs. The threat can, of course, be effective in curbing a misbehavior. But, at what cost to the student? And at what cost to the teacher?

The student can hardly be expected to focus more on the classwork. He or she must focus on gaining safety in the classroom, and, also, on keeping love needs satisfied. If keeping love needs satisfied means being "one of the guys" or "one of the gals," and that means continuing to "act out," then the student turns all his or her attention to the question at hand—how to pass notes more effectively and without getting caught. The lesson is now of very minor importance.

The teacher, too, is placed in some jeopardy. After all, calling the parents may be effective, but it is also an admission of minor defeat. It is the same as saying, "I can't control my classroom, so I need your help." If the behavior is so radical that this is necessary, this is certainly the right action for the teacher to take. But, if the behavior is only a minor annoyance, the teacher who makes a threat like "I'm going to call your parents," places herself or himself in as much jeopardy as the student.

More Effective Use of the Needs Scale

In keeping the focus on the lesson at hand, the teacher can make better use of Maslow's research. Insulting a student undermines the student's sense of warmth and friendship in the classroom. But the teacher can challenge the student to continue learning rather than threatening his/her "esteem-needs." A good response to a terrible answer might be: "I know you could find another answer to that question that would be more on target. Why don't you think about it while I call on a few other people. When you are ready, raise your hand again, and I will call on you."

This answer focuses the student's attention on improving the quality of the response. It does not set the student back to needing peer approval instead of teacher approval, or looking for some way to win back the teacher's friendship. It does not drive a wedge between teacher and student.

The same is true when disciplining students. Teachers should try to concentrate on the lesson and the student's innate need to self-actualize. Threatening responses only undermine these needs and force the student to a more

There is a great deal of difference, in student behavior and in our own behavior, between needing and wanting. We often want something badly, but do not really need it. There is a quick three-question test to tell whether something is truly a need or not. You can use it on yourself when you are tempted to buy that new pair of shoes or that irresistible video camcorder. Or you can use it to help students distinguish between behaviors that grow out of wanting and those that evolve from human needs.

1. If this urge were not satisfied, would physical or mental illness result?
2. If this urge were continually satisfied, would it reveal a deeper and more basic need?
3. Does physical and/or mental survival or growth truly depend on satisfying this urge?

primitive level. A better response to passing notes might be: "We really need your input to this discussion, and I know you can't give your full attention to thinking and passing notes at the same time. Why don't you consider the problem of thus-and-so, and raise your hand when you can help us to solve it?"

Only when this response is too mild should the teacher move down the level from self-actualization needs to love needs. Then the response might be to come close to the student, lean over and confide: "We have to share this classroom for the hour, and I find it very distracting when I see students passing notes. Could you try to stay with the class instead of passing notes?"

More to Come

There is more to come about this subject of "scaling" teacher responses to student actions in later chapters on discipline and management. For now, it is enough to note that teachers need to be acutely aware of the level of their responses to students, and to respond purposefully when moving students from sophisticated needs to more primitive needs. Just keeping this awareness active can make a great deal of difference in classroom behavior. *If you would like to judge your own responses, tape record your next class session, and later listen to your remarks as you interact with students. You will quickly get a feeling for the levels on which you are requiring students to respond.*

A model needs a chart

This chart is based on the work of Maslow and others. It divides needs into individual and societal hierarchies and shows the relationship of communication to the two domains of survival and growth needs.

[1]
Survival needs

[2]
Needs for Individual Safety and Self-Preservation.

[4]
Social Survival Needs

[3]
Needs for Individual Health

[5]
Needs for Adequate Interpersonal Communication

[6]
Needs for Individual Physical Growth

[8]
Needs for Physical Social Growth

[7]
Needs for Individual Emotional and Intellectual Growth

[9]
Needs for Societal Emotional and Intellectual Growth

[10]
Needs for Growth

Motivationally, man is a strange, if not bizarre creature: he is the only known organism to arise in the morning before he is awake, work all day without resting, continue his activities after diurnal; and even crepuscular organisms have retired to rest, and then take narcotics to induce an inadequate period of troubled sleep. But lest we decry man's motivational mechanisms, we should point out that without them we would not have the steam engine, the electric light, the automobile, Beethoven's Fifth Symphony, Leonardo da Vinci's undigested "Last Supper," gastric ulcers, coronary thrombosis, and clinical psychologists. Indeed, we might as well regard this aggregate as the human motivational syndrome.
—H. F. Harlow, "Motivation as a Factor in the Acquisition of New Responses," in *Curriculum Theory and Research in Motivation* (Lincoln, NE: University of Nebraska Press, 1953).

The Three Basic Learning Needs

Assuming that basic needs are met—the student feels physiologically well, feels safe in the environment, feels loved and cared for—new psychological needs arise. Among these are three that are especially important to learning. These three needs are the key to successful motivation—the key to getting students to want what you want in the classroom.

> Motivation is...the combination of forces that initiate, direct, and sustain behavior toward a goal. Goals are achieved by satisfying needs. Needs are the relatively permanent tendencies people have to be motivated in certain ways. The needs may be physical, such as for food, water, and safety, or they may be psychological. The three basic psychological needs ... are 1) the need to be an **active learner**; 2) the need to **socialize**; and 3) the need to **feel confident and secure**.[1]

Any learning activity which meets all three of these needs will succeed in motivating students.

Active learning

None of us likes to sit while someone else recites. Right now, you would probably rather be teaching than reading about teaching. This is natural. You have a need to be active. Likewise students need to exercise their instincts of origination through activity.

Socialization

Students also have a need to know one another. And, in Jewish education, which seeks to preserve Jewish society, we have this aim in common with the students—to insure that students meet and interact with one another. Generally speaking, this does not happen while chairs are in neat rows facing the teacher. Good motivation means providing opportunities for students to interact with one another, as well as with the teacher.

Confidence and Security

Last, students need to know that what the teacher requires is within the students' ability to achieve. Assignments and activities should be challenging, but never impossible. Students feel threatened when teachers ask the impossible. All their effort then goes to finding some way to feel safe again, rather than to learning. It's almost as if there is a

(1) Carl J. Wallen & LaDonna L. Wallen, *Effective Classroom Management.* emphasis added.

magical "comfort zone." It is a zone in which challenge is always present, but never overwhelming. Part of the art of motivating is knowing how much and what kinds of things your students can do.

Planning motivational activities

Just a moment ago, I made a sweeping generalization: *Any learning activity which meets all three psychological needs will succeed in motivating students.* Did you ask yourself: "Can he really be guaranteeing success?" If you did, you were doing exactly what I hoped you would do. This statement is actually a good example of what H. E. Aubertine calls "set induction."[2]

Set induction seeks to 1) focus student attention on the lesson, 2) create a framework for the ideas, principles or data which follow, 3) extend the students' understanding and/or application of abstract ideas through examples and analogies, and 4) stimulate student interest and involvement in the lesson.

Set induction is a technique which uses activities, stories, discussions, worksheets, games, or projects to ignite the lesson, encouraging students to take an active part in learning the content that follows. As a technique, set induction employs three basic sets: the orientation set, the transitional set, and the evaluative set. In essence, a set induction can be any action or statement by the teacher that is designed to relate the new content of the lesson to the common experience of the students. You can think of it as a bridge from what students already know to what you want them to learn.

Using Set Induction

To help explain how to use set induction, it is best to have some content in mind. Some years ago, I adapted a Hasidic story for use with nine-year-olds. The story was first told by Rabbi Simha Bunim. In brief, the story tells how a prince ran away with a band of gypsies. The gypsies loved the boy and taught him to dance. He performed as a part of the gypsy acting troupe, dancing with a bear. The prince's father sent a decree to all corners of the kingdom, asking that the prince be returned, and promising a reward. When, many years later, the gypsies learned that their dancing boy was the prince, they returned him to the king. The boy was overwhelmed by the trappings of the palace. His father, the king, was so pleased to see him that he offered to give the

School environments typically provide many kinds of rewards and punishments that are intended to motivate students such as grades, prizes, teacher and student approval. The devices the school uses to motivate are called *incentives.* In order to be effective in motivating students the incentives must provide some degree of need satisfaction. When teachers talk about motivating students to do school work, they are generally referring to the use of incentives. Yet, teachers should realize that motivation for learning is not something magically produced by the use of incentives, but a process involving complex conditions within the individual and the total school environment.
— Carl J. Wallen and LaDonna L. Wallen, *Effective Classroom Management.*

(2) H. E. Aubertine, "An Experiment in the Set Induction Process and Its Application in Training" (Ph.D. diss., Stanford University, 1964).

prince anything that his heart desired. The prince thought for a moment, and finally said, "I could use a new pair of dancing shoes." Bunim went on to explain that we are all like the prince when we stand in prayer before God. We are so overwhelmed by the trappings of glory that we forget to ask for the great things—like world peace—and pray instead for the little things that we could easily get for ourselves.

Using Set Induction to Introduce or Orient Students to a Subject

In using set inductions, make certain that you are planning for success rather than failure. Especially in the early phases of learning new material, it is important that there be a great deal of positive reinforcement. You must attempt to stay within the "comfort zone." Learning tasks must be balanced between conveying no challenge and being so difficult that the learner can only resign in frustration.

Examples: One way of motivating students before presenting this story would be to ask them to write down on a slip of paper the one thing they would ask for if they could ask for anything in the world. When everyone is ready (after a minute or two), tell the story.

Another way would be to ask the students to pretend that a king had just posed a great challenge to them. He wants to honor his son, the prince, who is just returning from a long trip. What kind of a gift could a king give to honor his child? Divide the class into small groups and ask each group to decide on an appropriate gift. When the groups are through (after five or six minutes), form the chairs into a circle and tell the story.

Analysis: In both cases above, the set induction is a bridge from what students already know to the content of the lesson. Also, the examples are informed by what we know of motivational techniques. In the first case, the motivation is active—calling upon the students to make a personal decision; and it is within the "comfort zone," because the decision is one which students can make from their own experience. The first instance, however, is not social.

The second example fulfills all three of the basic learning needs—it is active (students must think, discuss, and arrive at a conclusion); it is social (the decision is a mutual one in small groups); and it is within the "comfort zone."

Both are good motivating activities. Not every activity must fulfill every need in order to be successful. But the overall balance should be maintained so that every need is addressed each time the class meets. The teacher who chooses to use the first example should make provision for social activity elsewhere in the lesson plan.

Using Set Induction as a Transition

Examples: The teacher has just completed telling the story (omitting Bunim's conclusion) and now divides the class into small groups. Each group is instructed to decide what the prince could have asked for from the king instead of dancing shoes. Afterwards, the class moves its chairs back into rows and the teacher asks the groups to report on what they decided to ask for and tells what Simḥa Bunim concluded from the story.

Alternatively, the teacher tells the entire story, including the conclusion of Bunim. The teacher then passes out photocopies of the weekday *Amidah*, the nineteen blessings in which we ask God for things which are important to us as a people. The class is divided into small groups and the groups are instructed to make a list of the things the Jewish people has asked for through the ages.

Analysis: In both cases above, the teacher has provided for all three of the basic learning needs: both lessons are active, social, and within the students' grasp. In addition, they both use the story as a starting point. In doing set induction for transitions, the idea is still to move from what students know (or what they have just learned) to the next level of knowledge (or the remaining content of the lesson). As you will see next, set induction can also be used to help conclude a lesson.

Using Set Induction in Evaluation or Conclusion

Examples: The story and Bunim's conclusion have been discussed and analyzed. Now the teacher leads the students to think about the prayer service, specifically about the personal, silent prayer which follows the *Amidah*. What kinds of things will they ask for the next time they come to this personal prayer? Will they remember the lesson which Bunim taught? How can they apply this lesson? After a brief discussion, the teacher asks each student to write out a short, personal prayer.

The story and Bunim's conclusion have been discussed and analyzed. The teacher now asks the class as a whole to compose one prayer on the chalkboard. The teacher takes suggestions from anyone in class, and works toward the composition of a class prayer. When the prayer is completely written, the teacher either asks everyone to copy it down in their notebooks, or promises to copy it down and hand out photocopies of it the next time the class meets.

In transmitting the idea of set induction, there has been a tendency to emphasize its importance at the beginning of a lesson, and to relegate to minor importance its uses in transition and in evaluation or conclusion. This tendency reveals a weakness in the way many teachers and teacher trainers understand motivation.

Motivation is not a means of getting a lesson going. It is more like a life preserver to a drowning person. It must be present all the time, in every phase of a lesson, else the lesson can be relegated to Davy Jones' locker.

Analysis: Set induction as a conclusion or evaluation helps students to make the transition from the content which is learned in the classroom to the application of that content in their everyday lives. This is what is done in both cases above. Learning needs are still kept in mind. In the first example, the activity calls upon students to be active (in writing out their personal prayers), social (in discussing the implications of the story as a group), and well within the comfort zone. The second example lays more stress on the social aspect of learning, calling upon everyone to join in together in one activity. Since the final composition is the combined output of the group, it is surely within the comfort zone.

Summary of Set Induction

When using set induction to introduce a new lesson, the principal focus should be on how the new material relates to the everyday experience (the world) of the student. In structuring a transition, the same techniques are applied to show how a piece of the lesson relates to the next piece of the lesson. Still later, the same techniques can be used to make the lesson a part of the everyday experience or world of the student.

A lesson can also begin with a set induction which evaluates or concludes the lesson from the previous session. This, too, can be a way of "bridging" from what students already know to the next content to be learned. This is especially important in teaching subjects which tend to be serial or "stair-step" in nature, such as history and Hebrew.

As you work with set induction, and focus on creating activities which meet the three basic learning needs, you will find many more ways of using this technique. And you will want to include it in your lesson planning.

Success in Motivation

Planning for success in motivation is really relatively simple. It means (a) keeping the students attention directed to the lesson and its evolution, (b) insuring that activities and projects are carefully planned to meet the three basic learning needs, and (c) allowing students to do the real work of the classroom—learning.

Chapter 6
Behavior 101: Simple Techniques for Effective Classroom Control

In this chapter

Good teaching relies on good classroom management. Motivating students and presenting materials are both of little use if the students are not staying with the class. Teachers confronted with difficult classes often wonder how to change the class. Perhaps they are asking the wrong question. That's where this chapter begins.

Cybernetics includes a basic concept with valuable applications to classroom control. To begin with, cybernetics is not really a science, but a congeries of sciences which include the theory of information and its measurement, the concept of communication nets with variable characteristics, and the way in which such nets evolve an equilibrium.[1]

In plain language, cybernetics deals with how systems—of complex and simple organisms and machines—operate. We are interested here in what is sometimes called "the law of requisite variety." This law of cybernetics states that in any given system, the most flexible part of the system will eventually gain control.

Consider, for example, what is the most flexible part of the system we call the automobile? You can immediately eliminate the brakes, the steering wheel, the motor, and the gas pedal—each of these can be used to serve only one purpose. Without the other parts, each of them would be unable to operate the system—that is, drive the car. The most flexible part of the automobile "system" is the driver. The behavior of the driver is flexible enough that—no matter what other part of the system may control the automobile for a moment or two—inevitably control returns to the driver.

The classroom is a system, too. And the same law applies. The most flexible part of the classroom system will

(1) "Cybernetics" by Norbert Wiener in The *Encyclopedia Americana*, Grolier Inc., (Danbury, CT: 1982) Vol. 8, p. 364.

eventually control it. Consider this situation. A student is "acting out" in class by making a series of wisecracking answers to every question the teacher asks. The teacher attempts to stop this behavior by reprimanding the student. The student stops wisecracking, but begins whispering loudly "to his neighbor." The teacher persists in making the *same* reprimand. The student has become more flexible than the teacher. In such a case, the student will eventually control the classroom.

If, on the other hand, the teacher has a wider variety of choices than the student—if the teacher first laughs, then smiles, then frowns, then points an accusing finger, then whispers a cautionary message to the student, then changes the student's seat, then isolates the student from the other students, then changes the activity of the class so that other students can no longer concentrate on the disruptive student, then maneuvers the disruptive student into actively working on the matter before the class, then threatens the disruptive student with total isolation and extra work, and so on—the teacher can exhibit a greater degree of flexibility than the student. In such a case, the teacher will eventually control the classroom.

In any classroom, there is one individual's behavior that you as the teacher know you can always change—your own. Since it is far easier to learn to change your own behavior than it is to force students to change their behavior, it only makes sense that you can achieve the greatest degree of control over your classroom by achieving the greatest degree of control over yourself!

It boils down to this: If you wish to control the classroom system, you must become the most flexible part of that system. To do this, you need a variety of options for dealing with disruptive behavior on the part of anyone else in the system. The more options you have readily available to you, the more likely you are to remain in constant control. The teacher who runs out of options yells and screams to no avail.

That sounds simple, you may say, except for one thing—where do I get all these options? There are two possible answers. The first is that you make a list of options and keep the list nearby while you are teaching (until the list turns into patterned behavior, at which point you can throw it away).

But, you may say, what if the list is not long enough? This leads to answer number two: You can learn to develop options on the spot.

Teachers who develop options on the spot have the advantage of never being at more than a temporary loss for what to do. And, to a person, they all follow only one rule for developing these options: *If something doesn't work, they try* **anything** *else.*

Ready-made Options

Until you can go into the classroom equipped to be totally flexible, however, it is wise to go into the classroom armed with some ready-made options for behavior control. If you were in a university setting, this set of ready-made options might be called something like "Behavior 101." That's where we will start.

The secret is in "containing" any disruption at the lowest possible level—that is, before it escalates into a major problem. To do this, you must have a progression of interventions, beginning with the most minor kinds of suggestions and advancing slowly to a serious conclusion such as sending the misbehaving student out of the class to the office or to the library with an assignment.

In no case should you allow the student to engage you in dialogue, since this is always disruptive to the class. It suits the disruptive student more than it suits the teacher. Instead, your every maneuver should be aimed at keeping you in control—even if that means changing the lesson plan slightly in order to proceed without further disruption. Remember: If you stay flexible, you stay in control.

My suggestion is that you read each of the following possibilities, then make a list that suits you and feels comfortable to you. Keep the list nearby for a few weeks, or a few months, until you are certain that you have mastered it, and before long you will reach the point at which you will be ready to develop options "on the fly."

A Hierarchy of Interventions

1. **Make eye contact.** Your first choice is to hint that the behavior is unacceptable. Do this merely by letting the student know that you "have your eye on" him or her. This is an excellent first choice since it can be done while you continue the lesson—it requires no interruption of the class.
2. **Make eye contact and frown.** This could be a first choice for teachers who feel that number 1 is not strong enough even as a beginning. It is equally effective as a number 2, since there is still no need to interrupt the

As a teacher, I am the sum total of a large variety of methods and philosophies which I have absorbed and tested. These work for me. Sometimes, a thing may fit my philosophy perfectly but if I find that it does not hold true in the classroom, I cast it out on its ear.

The field of discipline or behavior-control is a primary testing ground. Generally, "experts" in this field fall into one of two categories—those who advocate a situational approach, and those who advocate some form of behavior modification.

After much trial and error, I am a devotee of the behavior-modification approach. Here are its advantages:

1. The approach, from first to last, is based on underlying principles. (Here, for example, the major principle is "containment.")
2. Since there are underlying principles, one can extrapolate to determine appropriate actions. (In the situational method, each situation must be analyzed individually in the search for one, optimum response. Here, we can see a general trend of action and thus never run out of options.)
3. The behavior-modification approach is proactive, dealing with problems before they become problems.

(By contrast, the situational people usually react to specific situations.)

There are those who call the professors of any education department that specializes in behavior modification as "rat men," referring to their proclivity for doing experiments with rodents. But this need not bother you overmuch. After all, in changing student behaviors you might say we are always involved with the problem of the behaviorists: how to pull habits out of rats.

Unlike the "bag of tricks" approach, the behavior-modification approach is founded on a sound basis—the tenets of behavioral psychology. In simple terms, it is based on the assumption that all behavior—both appropriate and inappropriate behavior—is learned. Those who strictly adhere to the principles of behavior modification assume that (1) a few basic processes such as positive reinforcement, negative reinforcement, punishment, and extinction account for learning at all age levels and under all conditions; and (2) learning is controlled largely, if not entirely, by events in the environment.
—James M. Cooper, *et al., Classroom Teaching Skills: A Handbook* (Lexington, MA: D.C.Heath and Company, 1977).

regular lesson or the class in order to let the student know that you "frown on this kind of behavior."

3. **Shake your head in a negative motion.** Once again, this requires eye contact, but is non-disruptive.

4. **Walk near to student. Invade student's "personal space."** All of us have a physical space around us we consider "personal space." When someone comes into this space without permission, it causes us to feel uncomfortable. This intervention is extremely effective—it is often the closing round in a student's disruptive behavior. It is most effective when the teacher continues teaching the lesson, even while pressing close to the disruptive student by leaning across the student's desk, or resting a hand on the back of the student's chair. It is low on the list of interventions because it requires no comment on the teacher's part, and requires no interruption of the class lesson.

5. **Address student in an aside,** with a simple "sh—" sound. This is the first of those interventions which cause very minor interruptions of the lesson. It is important not to allow this to be interpreted by the disruptive student as an invitation to dialogue. Make sure you do it quickly and firmly, and immediately continue the lesson.

6. **Speak rhetorically** to student, asking something like "Are you all right?" Again, do not allow this to be interpreted as an invitation to dialogue. The question is meant to give the student pause to think. It is meant to signify something like, "Aren't you embarrassed by this behavior of yours?" or "Don't you think there is something fundamentally wrong with disturbing the class in this manner?"

7. **Lean over close to student and ask student to take a seat "closer to you."** Remember, the purpose of all these interventions is to keep the level of the disruption as low as possible. With this intervention, we come to the point of actually taking a physical action. Even so, we want to make the interruption of the lesson as unobtrusive as possible. By speaking "privately" to the student, you avoid making him or her the absolute center of attention. The attention of the class focuses instead on your action. Notice, you still have not given the student any reason to verbally respond. If there is any response, you must try to avoid being tempted to

dialogue. The student who refuses to move the first time should be admonished with, "This was my suggestion. Remember that I made it." Nothing further is required. Any attempt to argue or fight with the student at this point would serve the student's needs but not your needs or the needs of the class.

8. **Approach student, speak quietly to student, and explain classroom rules.** If you have set rules for the classroom, this is a good time to remind the disruptive student of the content of these rules. Do it in a general fashion, including all the set rules of the classroom. Do it quietly, again to focus attention on your action, not on the student. Do not invite dialogue.

9. **Warn student,** "If you persist in this behavior, we will have to take other measures." This is the first hint of a threat. It is made more effective by the fact that what "other measures" is left up to the imagination of the student. Psychologically, one can depend upon the student to imagine a worst case scenario for that particular student. Therefore, this kind of threat is more serious than one which is more specific. In addition, this may be done from the front of the room—publicly, not privately—so it is a definite escalation of the intervention techniques to a new plateau. Notice, however, that it still does not invite any kind of dialogue.

10. **Consider changing the classroom activity.** It is a fact of life that it is much easier for a single student to disrupt a class when the attention of the entire class is focused on any one point—such as the teacher—than when the attention of the class is dispersed. At this point, consider reassigning the discussion or work to the class as a small group activity by dividing the class into groups of four or five. When the class is divided in this way, the disruptive behavior affects only one small group instead of the group as a whole. Also, when the class is divided this way, and you are certain that they are working, you have time to deal with the disruptive student one-on-one.

11. **Call disruptive student to your desk for a short lecture on behavior.** Explain the purpose of the class. Remind the student that disruptive behavior robs other students of valuable time. Remind the student that you will be forced to take serious measures if the disruptive behavior continues. This is best accomplished when the class is in small groups. Send the student back to work in his or her small group. Maintain a close observation of the group which includes the disruptive student.

The story is told of a professor who had taught for many years and who was giving advice to a younger colleague. "You will find," he said, "that nearly every class has one student eager to argue. Your first impulse will be to silence that student. I advise you to think carefully before you do. That student may be the only one listening."

12. **Dictate the terms of an "agreement"** with the student. Tell the student that you will make an agreement with him or her. If the student will agree not to disrupt the class any further, you will agree to take no further action against the student. You are "willing" to forget the matter entirely. This falls under the rubric of helping the student "save face." By making this mock agreement, you are, in effect, giving the student a second chance, and a way out of what may have become a nervously repetitive behavior pattern.

13. **Deprive the student of some privilege.** If there is available to you some classroom privilege, or normal group social activity, which can be withheld, this might be an appropriate time to exact this kind of minor punishment. Withholding a privilege is a lesser and generally more effective maneuver than imposing a punishment. The "privilege" could be any social activity—it might even be withholding permission for the student to return to the small group from which you extracted him or her, to "wait out" the activity alone. This minor isolation from the social group may be enough to curb the misbehavior. Remember, disruptive behavior is only disruptive to the degree that a social atmosphere exists to support or reject it. If one cannot remove the behavior, one can sometimes remove the group, just as when one cannot contain a fire by robbing it of fuel, the best procedure is to rob it of oxygen.

Isolation has a way of making class routine look more attractive. The purpose of isolation is to reduce the alternatives open to the disruptive student and bring the realization that he has only two choices: (1) to be in class and behave; or (2) to be [separate] and sit. While he is [separate] you are not going to hurt or reject him, which would let him rationalize his misconduct on the basis of his dislike for you.— Carl J. Wallen and LaDonna L. Wallen, *Effective Classroom Management.*

14. **Remove student to the back of the room.** This is a token of the complete isolation to come. Before taking the last few steps, the teacher can hope to stem the disruptive behavior by maneuvering the student into a position in which he or she will have to struggle mightily for attention. Please note that none of these interventions call for shaming the student in any way. This is an important point to remember in taking effective disciplinary action.

15. **Warn student,** in the hearing of the entire class, that if the behavior persists, you will send the student out of the classroom.

16. When all else fails, **send the student out of the class**. The destination should be one previously agreed upon by the principal and the teachers. It may be the principal's office, or it may be the library. It may also be agreed in advance that the student should be given some written assignment to do while in isolation, as a

replacement for the normal class work—otherwise the isolation may itself be a reward to the student. If this is the case, the teacher should have such an assignment ready at all times. As a matter of course, the assignment, in writing, should be given to the student without remark, along with the verbal instruction that it be completed and returned to the teacher the following week as a condition of readmittance to the classroom.

Assumptions About Behavior

As a teacher you can do yourself a favor by making certain valuable assumptions about student behavior *a priori*.

The first of these is difficult for any teacher to accept. The fact is that the most common reason for classroom misbehavior is the behavior of the teacher. Being unprepared for instance, nearly always leads to misbehavior by allowing unoccupied time. This, in turn, leads to *ennui*, especially on the part of brighter students—who are more capable of taking advantage of the vacant time, to the disadvantage of the teacher. Lesson one: always over-prepare, never under-prepare. This will lessen the amount of disruptive behavior in your classroom.

Second, no matter what form the disruptive behavior takes, you can be certain that it is the best behavior that the particular student feels is available to him or her at that moment. In general, the disruptive student is proud of his or her ability to disrupt effectively. You have the difficult job of persuading the student that this is inappropriate behavior without causing the student to lose face. The teacher who insults a student may repress the student for the moment, but has actually lost control over the student, sometimes forever.

Third, disruptive behavior is more often aimed at entertainment than at defiance of the teacher. You should try never to take disruptive behavior personally. This can only lead you to anger; and anger can only lead you to rash judgment and confrontation. Often, taking one minute to share a laugh with the class over one student's disruptive behavior can save many frustrating minutes of disciplinary action. Laughter is a great curative.

Fourth, disruptive behavior is always more effective when the teacher insists on having the class' attention all the time. Teachers who lecture, lead discussions, ask questions, and talk constantly from the front of the classroom have many more disciplinary problems than those who mix their

General Creighton Abrams once found his tank division completely surrounded by the enemy. The enemy sent a note asking him to surrender. He sent back a note saying, "Never." Then he called his soldiers together and said, "Men, we are faced with a unique situation here. For the first time in our campaign we can attack the enemy in every direction!"

Sometimes a teacher can feel surrounded, too. The trick is to be as positive as the General.

teaching techniques, allowing students to interact naturally in small groups, debates, dramas, arts and crafts projects, and the like. Students need socialization, and will seek it. If it is not provided by the teacher, they will provide it themselves to the detriment of the teacher.

Last, most disruptive behavior is of limited duration because most students are not chronic misbehavers. In fact, the number of chronic discipline problems is so few that one is not likely to run into more than two or three every ten years of teaching. Yet there are teachers who overreact, who treat every disruptive behavior as if the culprit was a chronic problem. The result of this kind of desperate treatment is generally a self-fulfilling prophecy. As students see the teacher overreact, they intuit that their disruptions are effective and they continue to experiment to see just how batty they can make the teacher. This is the fast road to teacher burn-out. Don't take it. There's no need. Surely, out of the sixteen interventions given above, you can choose six or seven that will help you to avoid overreacting.

(And—please excuse the repetition, but—most discipline problems have their origin in teacher behaviors. If you forgot, perhaps you should read this section again. As they say about the healing powers of chicken soup, it couldn't hurt.)

Teacher Behaviors

"Behavior 101" would conclude with a summary and a final exam. We will forego the examination, but here's a summary:

A. Be consistent. If you make a promise or a threat, keep your word. If the rule is set for the whole class, enforce it for every student equally.

B. Be rational. Don't overreact. And always remember that it is faster and more efficient to change your behavior than to attempt to change the behavior of another human being. Above all, be flexible. If something doesn't work, don't give up: Try *anything* else.

C. Be firm. Keep your temper, but make sure that students understand that you mean what you say. If you employ laughter, be sure that you make it clear as soon as the laughter is over that class is back in session and now the lesson must go on with no further ado.

D. Be caring. Don't insult a student in front of his or her peers. Don't treat students as inferiors. Make it clear that you sincerely care about the problems that have caused a student to disrupt the class—it's just that, during class time, your duty is to the class. After class, let it be known, you will be glad to discuss any problem or concern the disruptive student may wish to advance.

E. Be a teacher, not a psychoanalyst. Your task is to keep the class free of disruption. Therefore, entering into dialogue with any single student for any length of time is self-defeating. Keep all disciplinary interventions short. Maintain the lesson as far as possible throughout. Don't ever attempt to "save" a student at the cost of losing a class.

F. Be flexible. Remember the law of requisite variety. Having options will place you in firmer control than any fixed behavior. Without a human mind to guide it, the brake in a car is easily as dangerous as the gas pedal. And if something doesn't work: Try *anything* else.

Chapter 7

The Ten Commandments of Classroom Management

In this chapter

The purpose of all classroom management is to make it possible for the teacher to be more effective in the presentation of the curriculum material. Jewish classrooms share most of the problems and advantages of secular classrooms, though the content matter is different. But classroom management can also be directly related to teaching in the Jewish classroom. This chapter presents ten commandments (it already sounds more Jewish, doesn't it?) for effective classroom management in a Jewish setting.

A sage was walking down the road one day and came upon a man beating a donkey. "Why are you beating that poor animal?" asked the sage. "Have you no mercy?" "I am beating this donkey to get its attention," said the man. "Why don't you just talk to the donkey?" asked the sage. "I will," said the man, "just as soon as I get its attention."

This story is justly famous in educational circles. It is sad to observe, but this approach is followed in too many classrooms. Some teachers think they can psychologically, if not physically, beat a student into listening. Knowing that most classroom behavior problems are actually related to teacher behaviors and practices, we know, too, that what we really need in any classroom is options. We need to practice the rule of requisite variety. We need to be flexible. But more than that, we need to remember whose behavior we can most readily change in the classroom. There is a minute chance of changing students. But there is a high probability that we can change our own behavior.

These are the Ten Commandments of Classroom Management:

I.   Thou shalt say *no* sparingly.

II.   Thou shalt learn "*withitness.*"

III.   Thou shalt "*overlap.*"

IV.   Thou shalt not commit *target mistakes.*

V.   Thou shalt not commit *timing mistakes.*

VI.   Thou shalt negotiate movements *smoothly.*

VII.   Thou shalt maintain *momentum.*

VIII. Thou shalt keep the group *alert.*

IX.   Thou shalt hold the group *accountable.*

X.   Thou shalt focus on the *group.*

Before you read the rest of this chapter—which is a commentary and explanation of these ten commandments—you might wish to try a little self-test. Write these on a sheet of paper and beneath each commandment, make a note or two to explain from your own experience what it means.

The Ten Commandments of Classroom Management: A Commentary

I. Thou shalt say "no" sparingly.

Desist behaviors are actions the teacher takes in an effort to stop student misbehavior. Jacob Kounin, a master of classroom management, has done extensive field study in classroom discipline. His studies show that teacher desist techniques vary greatly, but no one technique seems superior to any other. In fact, all desist behaviors are *equally ineffective.*

For one thing, by the time a student misbehavior is established, it is generally too late to take effective action.

Also, the more often the teacher says "no," the less likely it is that saying "no" will be effective. Saying "no" eventually sets up a spiral toward maximum ineffectiveness.

Before teachers develop a systematic approach to classroom management, they tend to use personal influence or threats as management techniques. The trouble is, the more often a threat is made, the more rapidly a teacher's personal influence declines. Kounin's research indicates that threats and personal influence techniques are largely ineffective. They may work once or twice, but they follow a law of ever-diminishing returns.

What is more important, depending on force is wasteful of your personal influence. In Kounin's studies, it had a negative "ripple" effect on the rest of the class. When one student was threatened, nervous behaviors were exhibited by other students, including nail biting, shifting in seats, chewing pencils, and looking around. Nearly all students were distracted from the content of the lesson. And, in the case of teachers who used threats regularly, students found the teachers less likeable, and rated them less competent and less fair than other teachers in the school.

II. Thou shalt learn "withitness."

"Withitness" behaviors are actions that the teacher uses to communicate to students that he or she knows what is going on. Kounin determined that "withitness" is much more significantly related to managerial success than nay-saying. Teachers who demonstrate "withitness" have fewer and less serious student misbehaviors.

III. Thou shalt "overlap."

"Overlapping" behaviors are those by which the teacher shows that he or she is paying attention to more than one level of classroom activity at the same time. For example, one can be paying attention to the content of the material, and, at the same time, be aware of a developing behavior problem. The trick is finding ways of showing this to the class, especially, to problem students. When combined with "withitness," overlapping behavior is a strong element of classroom management.

IV. Thou shalt not commit target mistakes.

Target mistakes consist of blaming the wrong student or attempting to stop a very minor behavior problem. For example, take the case of cheating in the classroom.

In cheating, two (or more) students are generally involved. In every case, one student needs the information and thus initiates the aberrant behavior. There is also a student who is more or less innocently involved. This student already knows the information, and is being cajoled or coerced into participating in the aberrant behavior. In the nature of things, we very often detect the problem on the rebound—when the information is actually being given. We have a tendency to identify the innocent member of the cheating "partnership," even before we identify the initiating student. It is a target mistake to blame the person who is being cajoled or coerced. When we commit this error, we set up a situation which leads the more innocent student to embarrassment or blame. If we continue to regard this individual with suspicion, we even tend to reinforce the very behavior which we want to discourage. The student may decide to live up to the reputation we have pinned on him or her, since we continue to behave as if this is his or her normal operating procedure. Thus, we lead the student to "a life of classroom crime." And this is just the opposite effect of what we intend.

Just as in cheating, target mistakes can occur in connection with passing notes, giggling, talking during class discussions, and a dozen other behaviors—many of them quite minor.

Target mistakes cause more problems than they solve. It is therefore essential to pinpoint precisely who is to blame before taking any action. And just asking who started a misbehavior will not necessarily result in a satisfactory answer. It is better, from a classroom management point of view, to watch a misbehavior go by than to pin the blame on the wrong student.

V. Thou shalt not commit timing mistakes.

Timing mistakes occur when the teacher tries to discourage misbehavior too late—once the deviancy has spread or increased in seriousness. Kounin found that teachers who display "withitness" and "overlapping" are less likely to make either target or timing mistakes. Accurate timing of intervention and consistently accurate targeting are both more essential to good classroom management than any particular method the teacher may choose to ultimately handle deviant behavior.

VI. Thou shalt negotiate movements smoothly.

Smoothness in transitions is the first of two elements that have to do with initiating, sustaining, or terminating a classroom activity. It is essential that these movements not be jerky. As we have seen, one must carefully plan the manner and method by which classroom movement is to be accomplished. And the teacher must give complete and simple directions to aid the smoothness of the movement.

VII. Thou shalt maintain momentum.

Kounin showed that momentum in the classroom is fundamental to good classroom management. It is the second element in good direction of classroom activity. The opposite of momentum is slowdown. Momentum is the pace of activities; slowdowns are usually caused by teacher actions that impede the momentum of activities.

For example, small group activities are among the most practical for allowing students to process new information and new materials. But when a teacher allows the small group to linger beyond its useful time, small groups also afford an excellent breeding ground for deviant classroom

Using Personal Influence

Carl and LaDonna Wallen, in their excellent book on classroom management, suggest three ways that a teacher can increase his or her personal influence with students:

(1) always use the minimum level of personal influence necessary to achieve the desired result;

(2) build personal influence by knowing your students well and demonstrating that you respect them and care about them; and

(3) use means other than personal influence to direct student behaviors. Other methods include designing activities that are highly motivating, using small group work, and using peer influence wisely.

In the next unit, we discuss many options for the presentation of materials which include these techniques.

behaviors. The general rule is to conclude any activity when it is at its peak—before it begins to wear thin, and even before it is entirely completed. In this way, the teacher sustains the momentum of the classroom.

VIII. Thou shalt keep the group alert.

Especially during individual recitations, the teacher's responsibility is to keep the group focused on content. Techniques for maintaining group alertness are ways of involving the group (through questions, discussions, note-taking, etc.) at all times. Certainly, in the Jewish school, time is at a constant premium. Thinking of the time as a precious commodity can aid the teacher in this process, and assure that the group remains alert to the need to work steadily and efficiently.

IX. Thou shalt hold the group accountable.

Group accountability refers to the teacher's ability to make students aware in advance of what is expected of them. Especially when the class focuses on one person (during individual recitation, for instance) it is essential that all the students in the class know why they must stay involved.

Before beginning any activity, it is good to outline for the students what will be expected of them at the end. This may be an oral review, a test, a paper, a report, or any of a hundred other options for review and repetition. As long as the class knows in advance the purpose of the activity, there will be a natural tendency on the part of the class members to take the activity seriously, and to participate actively.

X. Thou shalt focus on the group.

The classroom, particularly the religious school classroom, is not an appropriate place for individual therapy or extended individual attention. The teacher's job is to focus on the group, to keep the focus from passing to any individual—student or teacher. It is essential that you not allow yourself to be drawn into any extensive cross-conversation with any single pupil. Cross-conversation, even if it is related to the content of the curriculum, tends to break down the classroom spirit, and to allow other students to lose focus. In turn, these other students may seek new outlets for their energy, particularly outlets which are deviant in nature, and ultimately destructive.

Kounin's study did not extend to the use of humor in the classroom, but humor can be an extremely valuable aid to other classroom management techniques. As the *Journal of the American Medical Association* once observed, "There isn't much fun in medicine but there's a great deal of medicine in fun"—and they should know! For anyone who may have forgotten, here is the operating manual:

"Enlarge the oral orifice both horizontally and vertically in such a way that its corners turn up sufficiently to reveal the incisors. Inevitably, this at least to some extent wrinkles the skin surrounding the lateral areas of the eyes. For a full effect, the eyes must reflect an inner glow."—M. Dale Baughman, Editorial in *Contemporary Education* (Terre Haute, IN: Indiana State University, Oct. 1969).

Using the Ten Commandments

In practice, these ten commandments soon become a way of classroom life. By memorizing them, and carefully observing your own behavior in the classroom, you can get a better idea of the kinds of deviant behavior which you are helping to create. In other words, you can find which sins are your worst sins. Of course, we all have faults in one or more of these areas. The purpose of the "commandments" is to help us identify the worst of these faults and remind us how we might move to correct them.

Give and Take in the Classroom

Klein* used college students as his confederates. He instructed them to first respond to lectures by a guest professor with positive behaviors—smiling, looking at the instructor attentively, etc. He asked them next to respond for a time with negative behaviors—frowning, looking out the window, shaking their heads, etc. Then, for a while, the students were asked to pretend to be neutral.

Klein recorded and analyzed the professor's verbal and nonverbal behavior in response to the students' behaviors. The guest professor's behavior reflected student behavior; positive when they were positive, negative when they were negative, and neutral when they were neutral.

In repeating this same experiment, and interviewing the guest professor afterward, another team of researchers found that the teacher who had positive responses from the students felt that he or she had done a good job. The teacher who received negative signals felt badly about teaching the class that day. In short, the students' attitudes can be almost as important to your sense of good teaching—and your rate of burn-out—as your own attitude. So it is important to insure as positive a classroom environment as possible. That's what the commandments are all about.

There is one last word to say about this matter of teacher influence in classroom management, but instead of saying it, I will let you discover it from the following anonymous quip: "It seems that no matter how you encourage students to tread the path of righteousness, they insist on following in your footsteps."

The Pefect Lesson

It is said that the great Rabbi Israel of the Ḥasidim, the Baal Shem Tov, could teach the perfect lesson. On Friday evenings, when the Sabbath service was over, he would enter a large room. At one end of the room, a table was set. On it were two enormous candelabra, and between them an open book, the mysterious *Sefer Yetzira*, "The Book of Creation."

*S. Klein, Student Influence on Teacher Behavior. *American Educational Research Journal*, 1971, Vol.8, pp. 403-421.

Any Ḥasid who had a problem that week would come into the large room and stand in front of the table. Then the Baal Shem Tov would speak to the group. And their problems would all be solved.

One Sabbath eve, as the Ḥasidim left the presence of the Baal Shem Tov, one turned to another and said, "I'm surprised that you and the others stayed tonight. After all, the Baal Shem Tov was speaking only to me."

"To you?" asked the other Ḥasid. "That's not possible. Everything the Baal Shem said was directed to me alone."

A third Ḥasid, overhearing this conversation, interrupted. "Don't argue: you are both mistaken. The Baal Shem Tov was actually speaking only to me."

Then a fourth Ḥasid spoke up, saying the same thing; and a fifth; and a sixth; and so on. Finally they all fell silent, for they realized what had truly happened.

At first glance it may seem miraculous that a teacher can address an entire group and have each individual believe that the lesson is a personal one. In fact, this is all a teacher can ever do. It is one of the great secrets of teaching.

We never really teach a group, or speak to a group. Each person carries away a different part of any message you give. And whatever part that individual carries away, that is the part meant for him or her alone to hear. Something far greater than ourselves brings us together to share classroom moments. And no classroom moment can ever happen twice. Every lesson has the potential to be the perfect lesson. Every teacher has the potential to be the master teacher. All you need to be taught is how to reach down inside yourself to the potential that you know you have, and how best to bring it out into the reality that we share.

Unit Two
Classroom Activities

In this unit

A classroom under control is just the beginning. For effective teaching to take place, the teacher needs as much flexibility in presentation of materials as in management. This unit features an analysis of more than one hundred and twenty classroom activities with wide classroom applications.

Chapter 8
Reading, Writing, and Comprehension

In this chapter

Among the most common exercises in the religious school (along with arts and crafts), are exercises which use reading and writing as their basis. This chapter includes twenty-seven major divisions of such activities, along with many suggestions for use and implementation.

I began with an excellent list of teaching activities compiled by Toby Kurzband for the Jewish Community Center of White Plains. Through the years, I developed my own list for teaching and for my workshops. It now has a shape I find useful.

You can develop a similar process by keeping notes as you use these and other activities in your classroom teaching. Over the years, you will find yourself creating a personal list. And that list will become your constant reference as you plan your teaching.

Reading Activities

Reading may be assigned for pleasure or for information.

It is a myth that students do not read. Actually, most Jewish students (and, in my experience, most students in general) read all the time. The real questions are *what, when,* and *for whom* do they read??

Teachers often discourage reading by assigning lengthy or difficult passages, or by not assigning reading in a challenging and interesting way. The worst case is, of course, the most common: "For next time, read the next chapter." This makes reading sound like a dull, mechanical task.

But reading can provide excitement, entertainment, enlightenment, and growth. Ergo, there must be ways of making it sound, feel, and look interesting, even tempting.

Here are a few sample techniques I use:

[In some] classrooms, reading consists of repetitive practice of word recognition skills followed by blank filling in workbooks or on dittoed worksheets. There is no opportunity for children to apply their skills in reading for pleasure or for information. Oddly, it is most often the poor reader...who is taught reading as drill and skill and who rarely, if ever, gets a chance to apply his skills. Yet it is this learner who is least likely to be provided at home with opportunities to read for enjoyment. If our goal is children who are readers rather than children who can read, we must allow children to read. This seems almost too obvious to mention, but in many instances children are learning the mechanics of reading without applying them. Little wonder that some children do not see the objective of learning to read as being worthwhile.— Daniel Tanner and Laurel Tanner, *Curriculum Development.*

Reading for data

Most assignments for text reading are meant to prepare students for classroom work. This means the reading is important—perhaps essential—to the success of the classroom. The curriculum makes that clear. The teacher knows that. All that's left is to ensure that the students know it, too. The basic key to assigning reading for information is making the reading important from the students' point of view. The first step is conditioning the students.

Making students want to read.

The classroom science of behavior modification provides a technique for "conditioning" or habituating students to do what they might otherwise resist doing. This conditioning relies on prompting and rewarding appropriate behavior. As you (the trainer) proceed through each step of the conditioning, you must reward the students for completing the previous step. In this way, students first read to receive their reward from you. (The reward is generally nothing more than approbation.) As time progresses, the reading becomes a habit, and the new reward becomes the rich returns afforded by reading itself.

Like much classroom work, this method involves a degree of manipulation. Some teachers immediately feel uncomfortable at the idea of manipulating students. Manipulation has a negative connotation in our free society. But all education is, in essence, a form of manipulation. There is no reason to worry that you are "too much in control." As long as your manipulation is altruistic and not exploitative, it will be beneficial to the students.

Here is the conditioning process in brief:

1. Begin with a short assignment—a paragraph or two at most. Try to find exceptionally interesting material for the first assignment, and be *absolutely certain* that this material will be used as the basis for the next in-class discussion.

2. Try to find an exciting or particularly interesting piece of writing in the text.

While it might be argued that it is not the domain of the religious school to teach children reading, it is certainly the domain of the religious school to teach children to love Jewish reading—and that entails loving reading! And, if that is true of the religious school, it is doubly true of the day school and Hebrew school.

3. Look for a piece of writing which logically concludes in the paragraph or two *after* the paragraphs you will assign. Students will find it hard to resist reading an extra paragraph or two the first time, so most students will think they are "over-prepared." This feeling of over-preparedness can, in itself, provide a motivational reward.

4. Reward the first reading task by *referring* to the assigned reading the next class period.

5. Reward the first reading task by actually *opening* the text in the next class period. Ask students to locate a sentence or two within the assigned reading to illustrate some point being made in the discussion. In this way, the students will understand that the text and the content of the class are truly integrated and interrelated. And they will be rewarded with the feeling of having done something contributory to classroom success.

6. As the class term progresses, continue the process by repeating steps 1-5. Continually assign slightly larger chunks of reading matter. Always review the assigned reading matter explicitly and directly in the very next session. Try not to say, "It is in the textbook" or "It was in your reading assignment." Instead, instruct students to open the textbook in class and refer to specific sentences and phrases. This is imperative because it constitutes the real reward for students' being prepared—being able to use gathered information in a practical sense.

7. I repeat: *The most important element in this progressive reading/conditioning technique is that you use the textbook in class whenever you review the reading assignment.* If you (as the trainer) stop referring to the textbook in class, you will find that student preparation soon loses its luster, and students begin to slide off the mark. It is an unfortunate fact of life—well-known to behaviorists—that the deterioration of good reading and preparation habits takes place at a far greater rate than their attainment.

Making the reading important.

At one and the same time, reviewing the text in class and referring to the text directly both aid the teacher in modifying student behavior, and tend to make reading itself important. We can go several steps further in this regard, too. Initiate reading assignments by stating the purpose of the assignment. Make the purpose an objective or goal for the student.

1. Assign a problem that can be solved by reading the assignment.

2. Assign a question that can be answered by reading the assignment.

3. Explain how a given set of facts or logical operation will make more sense once the assignment is read.

Reasons to Read

Here are five corollary strategies for motivating students to read:

Strategy 1: Point out an uncertainty or ambiguity and ask students to read for the solution.

Strategy 2: Tell a part of a story or event and ask the students to read to fill in the missing portion(s).

Strategy 3: Ask students to read from a point of view (for example, as if they were historians, as if they were psychologists, as if they were reporters, etc.).

Strategy 4: Ask students to tell what they already know about a subject, then ask them to predict what they might learn by reading the selection.

Strategy 5: Ask students to read in order to prepare to teach the material in a specified setting (for example, to teach it to the rest of the class, to teach it to a younger class, to teach it to their parents, etc.).

4. Show how the reading being assigned is a logical extension of the reading that has previously been done.

Reading for pleasure

Most teachers imagine they are struggling upstream just to get students to read. It is easy to forget that literate people read because they want to read—for pleasure. "Pleasure"-reading does not mean only "light" reading. People often read difficult or technical material purely for pleasure. There is no reason that the classroom teacher should fail to capitalize on this propensity.

Some years ago, I thought of writing a book called, *Using Textbooks Effectively*. I wondered: Who knows the most about motivating people to read? From my own experience, I could see that for most teachers this was a lost art. But I did identify one segment of the populace that has maintained this art: librarians. I spoke to librarians and read books they recommended on library science.

You can use some of the library techniques listed below in motivating students to read textbooks—even though these techniques are used mainly to stimulate reading for pleasure. The line between the two is not as difficult to traverse as many imagine.

The Synagogue Library.

Most synagogues have a library. Some are fortunate enough to have an excellent library. Some are lucky to have an excellent volunteer or staff librarian. Others have a library in disarray, or a library in need of rejuvenation. In any case, it is almost unheard of for a synagogue to exist without some kind of library—even if it is only the books on the rabbi's shelves. From the time students enter the religious school, they should be encouraged to use the library.

Good librarians generally know and use specialized techniques to interest students in reading for pleasure. Among these are story—hours, miniature book reviews, personalized suggestions, and so on. If a competent person is available in your library, you will do well to watch him or her at work with your students.

If you do not have a librarian, you will have to be a "substitute librarian" for your students. In this case, you might wish to visit a librarian at your local public library to chat about techniques on a professional-to-professional basis.

For what reason other than economy of space are books displayed with their spines out? The spine of a book, with its Dewey decimal notations, is no more attractive than any other spine with such markings would be. And yet we expect the...child, who relates to very little through words, to relate to books through words printed on their spines.

This is the same child, remember, who is *always* attracted to pictures, whether found in comic books or on the television screen. Why then do we not make the most of his tastes and predispositions...? School

Regularize class visits to the synagogue library. Occasionally, you can shift some small-group work, story-telling, creative writing, and other class activities to the library itself. Encourage students to browse the shelves, choose books, and check them out. Encourage the synagogue to keep the collection current. Reading reinforces reading. And reading for pleasure nearly always leads to reading for information.

A Classroom library.

It is not always practical to visit the synagogue library. Nor does the synagogue library always include extensive resources on the particular content area of your instruction. Not only that, but most synagogue libraries do not systematically provide for putting books "on reserve" for a particular class.

The best solution is to maintain a small classroom library as a supplement to the synagogue library. The classroom library—one or two shelves in the back of the room—should include books directly related to your area of instruction. But the books need not be on any particular reading level; in fact, you should attempt to choose books on every conceivable level. If the grade being taught is grade five, the books might be on reading levels from grade two to adult. They can be used as quick cross-references to the textbook, as references for students preparing special reports, as extra credit reading for students who wish to learn more, as read-aloud books for story-telling time, as reading for pleasure during slack times, and so on. Old textbooks can be put to valuable use as the cornerstone of any classroom library. Likewise, old magazines and periodicals are good additions to classroom libraries. Some subjects also lend themselves to the development of a "horizontal file" in the classroom in which pictures, student reports and the like can be collected for later use.

There are two cases in which such classroom libraries are particularly important. One is the early childhood classroom and the other is the Hebrew language classroom.

The early childhood classroom. Young children love to hear stories. And they love nothing more than to hear their favorite stories repeated time and again (until the point where they have virtually memorized every word). They also love to peruse every picture in a picture-book. And they like to see and hear different versions of the same story, too. (There must be, at any given time, twenty or thirty versions of Noah and the Ark in print in picture-book form.) The best way to insure that they will read for pleasure is to make available the picture books and easy readers that they need on a permanent basis in the classroom. Then these can be used for free time, for story-telling time, as a basis for classroom dramatics, as a resource during classroom arts and crafts projects, and for children who wish to take them home to share with their parents. The classroom library should be a regular feature of all early childhood classrooms at the least.

The Hebrew language class. Similarly, nothing gives a student greater pleasure than using what has been learned. In Hebrew language instruction, a classroom library can make available other textbooks, ancillary readers, and supplementary reading materials on a level equivalent to that being taught. These can be used for further reading practice, for comparison reading, for ad-hoc testing, for classroom dramatics, and for a myriad of other purposes that can enrich the Hebrew language program.

Writing Activities

There are so many kinds of writing, and so many useful activities which involve writing, that no list could possibly be comprehensive. The following twenty-five examples give just a taste of what is possible in the classroom.

Essay

The rule with regard to assigning essay topics in the classroom is fairly straightforward. Always try to make the subject of an essay personal. This allows students room to give their opinions, as well as giving them reason for reviewing the basic facts of any subject matter. You can begin assigning essays as soon as children have learned to write. Also, allowing language students to write essays in simple Hebrew provides good exercise in vocabulary, dictionary use and language usage.

Biography

Students can write short biographical sketches of famous people, biographies of their parents and family members, and biographies of people they interview. All of these can be worked into the curriculum without a great deal of difficulty. Biographies give students the opportunity to seek role models with which they can easily identify.

Reasons to Write

Here are five additional strategies for encouraging students to write:

Strategy 1: *Set up a "book bindery."* Use a card table, or an extra classroom table, and place on it staplers, brads, hole punches, ribbon, cardboard, scissors, etc.— all the materials students need to "bind" what they have written.

Strategy 2: *Set up a "Poet's Retreat."* Use floor pillows or bean bag chairs to make one corner of the classroom a place for budding poets to find their muse. You might include a standard dictionary, a rhyming dictionary, some paper and pencils, some simple Jewish poetry anthologies (for example, some of the many books by Danny Siegel), a three-ring binder in which completed poems can be inserted for all to read, and even a small box of index cards with some suggested titles or subjects.

Prayer

Composing prayers is not an activity reserved for classes in Jewish liturgy. Many subjects in the Jewish school center on values which can be expressed in prayer language. And, as students become more comfortable with phrasing their beliefs in prayer, they become more comfortable with prayer and the Jewish prayer service itself. There are many permutations of Jewish prayer forms, allowing for a great number of diverse writing assignments. (For a description of these forms see *When a Jew Prays*, Behrman, 1973, chapter four.)

Radio or TV Program

The format of current radio and television news and news special reports is well-known to students by the time they reach grades three or four. Since, these are a part of the everyday "reality" of the children, asking the students to write scripts mimicking these programs appears to the students as "relevant." More importantly, from the point of view of the teacher, it may evoke opportunities for continuing interesting written activities into dramatic, filmic, and other modalities.

School or Class Newspaper

In skilled hands, planning and executing a class or school newspaper can be one of the most exciting and involving means of teaching. Newspapers afford many varied activities which match the many interests of students. And, a newspaper can be planned and executed around any time period and any subject. (Some years back, an Israeli company published an excellent series of "newspapers" entitled *Chronicles of the Past* based on biblical history.)

Newspapers can be a) large projects, stretching over many class periods and forming a unit; b) small-group projects meant to be accomplished in a shorter time; or even c) projects to be done individually as homework or in class.

Be certain to include the full range of written newspaper possibilities when suggesting what can be done: articles, editorials, columns, features, comics, sports, classified advertising, general advertising, movie reviews, book reviews, and more.

Don't be afraid to use this as a motivating technique more than once. It is almost always effective when it is introduced with proper enthusiasm and when you allow a great deal of latitude, especially for humor.

Strategy 3: *Set up a class "Mail Box."* Make a large mailbox from corrugated cardboard cartons. You can decorate it to look like a U.S. Postal Service box, or you can make it look like an Israeli post box. Be sure to include the "Pick-Up Times" on a label on the front, and a notice that says, "No Pick-Up or Delivery on Shabbat." You can ask the class to elect a postal clerk and you can design a rubber stamp and have it reproduced for a couple of dollars to be used from year to year. Then let the class write letters—to each other and to you. And have some fun with it.

Strategy 4: *Set up a "Detective Bureau."* Use an old file cabinet or desk, if you can get one. Set up a series of file folders with "clues"—they can be business cards, scraps of paper with writing, scraps of material, etc., and a partial story for each set of clues. The stories can come from the Bible, from Midrash, from folklore, or from your imagination. Students can suggest "solutions" to the mysteries and write out the scenarios as they see them.

Strategy 5: *Set up a "Bus/Rebus Stop."* Put up a cardboard bus stop sign in a classroom corner, labeling it "Bus/Rebus Stop." Have a few prepared rebus- tyle puzzles on hand, pencil and paper, a two-tiered paper tray with one tier labeled "In" and one tier

labeled "Out," and lots of storybooks. Ask students who visit the center to pick up a rebus from the "In" tray and to leave behind a new rebus in the "Out" tray.
reworked from ideas found in Imogene Forte, et al., Cornering Creative Writing.

Distributing the newspaper can be almost as much fun as creating it. It can be a way of raising funds for tzedakah projects, of sharing classroom progress with parents and peers, or just of sharing written work with all the members of the class. If the newspaper was compiled over a long period of time, and "officers" were appointed or elected for various purposes, be sure to include a masthead listing the names of the "editor," "features editor," and so on. If not, be sure the newspaper has a proper masthead and simply list everyone who was involved. And always remember to place a date and class in the newspaper for future identification.

In advanced Hebrew language classes, newspapers provide a stimulating writing and comprehension exercise for building dictionary, vocabulary, and usage skills.

Letters

Using letter-writing as an activity can place practical emphasis on any subject matter taught in the classroom. Depending on the content of the curriculum, letters can be addressed to members of the synagogue board; pen pals in Israel, Russia, other synagogues, etc.; members of Congress; newspaper editors; parents; etc. Letters can be composed by individuals, or—especially in the lower grades—can be composed by the class as a whole (with each child making and signing a copy from a master letter on the chalkboard).

In Hebrew classes, letters are excellent skill-builders.

Outlines

In the middle grades, students are typically taught outlining as a part of their general school curriculum. Many a traditional teacher uses outlines as an activity to reinforce (and enforce) homework, reading for data, and other classwork. Outlining can be used in many other ways, too. Students can outline future writing projects, results of small-group work or research, library work, and countless other things. Students individually, or the class as a whole, may also outline difficult concepts, breaking them down into their component facts and ideas for clarity. Last, but not least, outlining is one of the writing activities which can be effectively done using the chalkboard.

Dictionary

Most Hebrew teachers ask students to build a personal dictionary as their vocabulary increases. But creating a dictionary of terms and ideas is a good activity in almost any unit of instruction. Since most teaching in the religious school includes Hebrew value-words and phrases, the dictionary can also help to integrate general Jewish studies with Hebrew language studies. Dictionaries are not just for students who are already good writers and readers. Younger students can copy words from the board and draw pictures or symbols beside the words to identify them. Dictionaries also provide a means of reviewing what has been covered in a unit of teaching and a source for testing materials.

Quiz or examination questions

Asking students to compose test questions is a good writing challenge, especially toward the end of a unit of teaching. It helps students to identify the main ideas and concepts learned, and allows students to feel like full participants in their own testing process. In addition, it makes testing seem less like a punitive measure, and more like what testing ought to be—a diagnostic and reinforcing technique.

Some teachers collect test questions composed by students and use them as the basis for creating the actual tests given to the class. This has the advantage of making testing more personal and relevant to the class as a whole.

It is good to give students options in the writing of their test questions. Some questions can be written calling for essay-type answers, but many more should be written as multiple-choice, true and false, and short-answer items. It is helpful, especially when first using this technique, to provide some examples of each kind of question—either writing these examples on the chalkboard or preparing a handout for the students—as a basis from which the students can work. This technique can be used from middle grades upward and in the Hebrew language class, but tends to be difficult for early learners.

Case study

Many topics lend themselves to the writing of case studies. A case study is a brief sketch of an actual situation involving a specific group, family, or individual. It can be written in an imaginative sense from gathered data (for example, a case study of a Jewish family living in France at the time of the Napoleonic emancipation of the Jews might show in microcosm how the emancipation affected the lives of Jews of France as a whole), or it can be written from actual biographies or histories (as, for example, a case study depicting Benjamin of Tudela's visit to one specific community).

Summaries

Writing summaries of lessons or units of teaching can help students paraphrase new learnings. Asking small groups to compose summaries of their work to be later shared as handouts can be a way of completing small-group work without the usual tedium of having each group make a report while the other groups listen. Students can be asked to write summaries of books they have read for pleasure or for information. Summaries of encyclopedia articles and other reference reading can be used as a basis for beginning classroom discussions.

Riddles, Jokes, Puns

From the early middle grades, students often take delight in riddles and jokes. Beginning in the middle grades, most students also enjoy puns (which some experts consider the highest form of humor; others consider them the lowest). Asking students to phrase what they have learned in the form of humor challenges them to actualize their understanding of the material. Much depends here on the class and its particular composition, but for most groups, riddles, jokes, and puns can be not only relaxing, but also instructive.

Story

The short story allows for in-depth creative thinking. It is usually considered an activity best-suited to individual assignment. There are forms of story-writing which can, however, be used in small-group work. A popular word-game in which one person begins a story, the next person continues it, and so on, can be adapted to written form, if the subject matter under discussion lends itself to this. Schools and teachers can also offer prizes or publication for voluntarily-submitted short stories (and poems, essays, songs, etc.). In assigning stories, it is recommended that a theme be the central focus of the assignment.

Poem

Beginning with the youngest children, simple poems can be written by the class as a whole, with the teacher writing them on the chalkboard. By the middle and upper grades, students can be encouraged to keep poetry journals and to use poetry as a form of self-expression related to the themes being discussed in the religious school. In any creative writing assignment, poetry can be an alternative to stories or essays.

In addition, poetry has a number of classical forms—sonnet, lyric, haiku, etc.—among them some very Jewish forms such as the psalm and the *piyyut,*—which make for interesting activities. When assigning a form to young people, it is best to photocopy an example or two to discuss first. Try to choose as an example a poem whose subject relates to the content of the curriculum. Ask students to make notes on their copy of the example as the class discusses how the particular poetic form is constructed. Also try to clarify how meaning is conveyed by the poet; and, if you can, how poetry differs from other forms of creative writing (its personal perspective, its general brevity, its innuendo, its multidimensionality, and so on).

Because poetry is personal and can be brief, it is usually the creative writing assignment which students most enjoy. Surprisingly (or is it?), most teenagers enjoy writing poetry, though they may sometimes be shy about sharing it openly.

Play

Writing a play can be a class effort, a small-group activity, or an individual exercise. It can be the beginning of a larger unit of study which might well culminate in a dramatic performance for the class, school, family, or community. Playwriting forces us to think in three-dimensional models. Dialogue, character creation, character development, costumes, scenery, stage directions, lighting, and so on, are all a part of the play-writing process. When the play is complete, it must also be practical—that is, it must be feasible to stage it, though it need not actually *be* staged.

In early grades, plays can be written for the narrator and actors who are silent. The teacher or a good reader can then "act" the narrator, reserving the many parts for the students. This technique, of course, can be used without regard to the students' age level. But older students can write much more sophisticated scripts without much trouble. Small groups can script plays for just the four or five characters in the group.

Plays can be of the one-act variety when the assignment is time-restricted; or of the full-blown three-act or five-act varieties for whole units of teaching. They can be composed in a relatively short period of time, or developed scene by scene over a longer period of time.

In this section of the activity cycle, we are more interested in the scripting of the plays than the actual presentation, which we shall discuss later.

Words to a song

Another popular activity is writing lyrics for songs. When the purpose is to exercise creativity in the written word, the melodies used can be those of familiar songs—*O My Darling, Clementine; I've Been Working on the Railroad; Blue Moon; Adon Olam; David Melech Yisrael;* etc. Alternative lyrics can also be provided for tunes of popular television commercials or popular theme music. This shortens the time needed to concentrate on melody and rhyme placement; and allows students to have more latitude in their writing of lyrics.

Song-writing can be communal or individual, depending on the purposes of the exercise. It is a good class activity for a group which exhibits rowdiness, because it gives them a chance, as a group, to "let off steam."

Ads or TV commericials

Writing advertising, such as that which might be found in a newspaper; or writing scripts for advertising which might be heard on radio—or heard and seen on television—provides a short assignment in creative writing. It can be used to move students in progression toward longer assignments—song-writing, poetry, stories, essays—or on its own. It lends itself to a wide variety of situations common in the religious school, especially in conjunction with the study of tzedakah organizations. Good "commercials" for radio and television might be recorded on cassette and videotape respectively. They might even be played on the school loudspeaker, or just for the enjoyment of the class, or as a feature on parent visitation day.

Diary

One of the simplest creative writing assignments is asking students to keep a diary. It can be a diary of thoughts they have toward the end of each class session (if you give them a few minutes at the end to compose their thoughts) or a diary of the class itself. It can be the imaginary diary of an historical figure or a figure from a particular period of history, or even a "personal" diary in which the student places himself or herself in the midst of an historical event. Before beginning diaries with students, it is recommended that you make clear to them exactly how much you expect of them (one line, one paragraph, one-half page, one page per session, etc.). Some students will undoubtledly do more, but there should be a class understanding as to what is minimal.

Diaries may be regularly collected and read by the teacher, considered the personal property of the student, made the center of a "sharing" period from time to time, or selectively read aloud by students. If the teacher is the main reader, he or she should make responsive comments in the margins of the pages to reflect the fact that the reading has been thoughtful. This process of diary and comment can become a form of dialogue with the students. It will certainly reflect the teacher's personal interest in the lives and thoughts of his or her students. If it is to be done, however, it is very important that the teacher make it known in advance so that students will phrase their thoughts appropriately and not feel offended or personally-invaded by the teacher's reading.

Slogans

Developing slogans in conjunction with curricular content actively allows for the paraphrasing of major points made in the classroom. Slogans are generally created individually or in small groups, with the results being shared or honed by the class as a whole. The object of the exercise can be to develop one "best" slogan or a number of appropriate slogans. The teacher can provide examples of slogans from advertising campaigns, dictionaries of quotations, and other sources to get the class started. Judaism contains a number of such slogans, the best-known being the slogan of the Maccabees, "Whoever is for the Lord, follow me," and David's very effective campaign slogan, "Saul has slain his thousands; but David has slain his tens of thousands.

Lists

Many subjects lend themselves well to the compilation of lists. Lists may be compiled as a one-time activity, or kept throughout the class term. I used what can be considered a good example of a list-keeping activity in the summaries at the end of each chapter of *Israel: Covenant People, Covenant Land*. (UAHC, 1985) Working on the premise that the covenant between God and Israel developed through the ages in incremental fashion, I asked students to continually add to their definition of the covenant a list of the new and salient points made in each chapter. To do this, they had to evaluate what in each chapter related specifically to the covenant. It thus allowed them to build a list-*cum*-definition which would afford them a perspective on the course as a whole when it was completed. Most courses include some content which progresses incrementally and can become the subject of a list.

A Values Shopping List

One kind of list you can encourage students to write is a "values shopping list."

Prepare a list of all the values that you are teaching through the year's curriculum and try to keep each value to one or two words. Then number a shopping list from one to ten and ask students to choose the ten values they most want for themselves from the "Values Supermarket."

Alternatively, just suggest that a "Values Supermarket" exists, and ask students to list the things they think would be on the shelves that they would want specifically to choose for themselves.

Values shopping lists can help make the meaning of what you are studying clear to your students.

Lists can also be compiled in a more "imaginative" way. For example, one might make a "shopping list" for the priests building the Tabernacle, or a "things-to-do-today" list for a Jew about to be expelled from Christian Spain in 1492.

Book review

In conjunction with reading for pleasure—or even reading for information—students can be encouraged to do book reviews as creative writing projects. Experienced secular teachers usually provide a one-page form for this purpose with spaces for author, title, publisher, copyright date, main ideas, a short summary, and a personal opinion. This kind of form helps both the reader and the teacher to be sure that the book review accurately reflects the book which was read.

Though book reviews are generally based on actual reading, a fun permutation is to ask students to create reviews of books which do not really exist, but which might have been written. What if Bar Kokhba had written an autobiography? What if a book about women in the shtetl had been written by a shtetl housewife? And so on. Creating assignments such as this can also test the creativity of the teacher—and that's worthwhile, too.

Book reviews are generally individual projects, but in those instances when the entire class reads one book, a class review or small-group review can be compiled.

Epitaphs

Jewish epitaphs follow a general format—for details, see the *Encyclopedia Judaica*, or *The Complete Book of Jewish Observance* by Leo Trepp (Behrman, 1980). [Which is interesting in and of itself.] The Jewish epitaph form can also be a good way of briefly paraphrasing and summarizing biographies which have been read, or the lives of heroes and heroines who have been studied. Provide an example for the class to study together at the beginning of the assignment. Explain the use of the epitaph. And also explain what keeps epitaphs from being merely morbid.

Responsa

The responsum is a uniquely Jewish writing form. (For a complete description, see the *Encylcopedia Judaica* article, "Responsa.") The idea is startlingly simple. As a question, issue, or problem arose in the diaspora—especially in a place where rabbis were scarce (or, if the question was especially difficult, where the opinion of a great rabbi was desirable)—a letter of inquiry was written and posted. The rabbi to whom the letter was addressed would consult law codes, the Talmud, and other sources, and prepare a detailed written response which was then posted to the community in need of advice. The interchange often gave rise to emendations in custom or new interpretations in law which might become binding not only on the community which posed the query, but on general Jewish observance.

Examples of the responsa form can be readily found in synagogue libraries, collections of Jewish writing, and Jewish textbooks. Usually, only the answer was preserved for posterity, but the question can easily be inferred from the response. Before asking a class to prepare responsa, the whole concept should be discussed using an actual example or two.

The class can prepare either the query or the answer as an activity. If a query is prepared, it can be sent to the synagogue rabbi for his response. Or small groups of students can pose questions to one another. If a respose is expected, the question can come from the material studied and can be posed by the teacher.

The responsa format encourages students to do research and to insert quotations from books, articles, and interviews. It therefore lends itself to use by older students, from the later middle grades up.

Ethical wills

Ethical wills are a typically Jewish form of creative writing. In the Middle Ages, when Jews had little physical wealth to pass from generation to generation (and when the greatest Jewish wealth was measured in terms of Torah and learning) it became customary for Jews—especially scholarly Jews—to leave detailed sets of instructions to their progeny. The instructions concerned themselves with the best ways to live, the values to which future generations should adhere, and personal observations about the meaning of life and the meaning of Judaism. These were ethical wills. (For a more thorough discussion, see the *Encyclopedia Judaica*.)

Students can begin working on ethical wills now. Teenagers can advise the next generation of teenagers what they have discovered about life so far. Adults can think in terms of the next generation of Jews, and what advice should be handed down to them. The ethical will can also be an exercise in imagination: What kinds of things would Elijah have said in an ethical will? What kind of ethical will could Alfred Dreyfus have written? And so on.

If they can by any means contrive it, my sons and daughters should live in communities, and not isolated from other Jews, so that their sons and daughters may learn the ways of Judaism. Even if compelled to solicit from others the money to pay a teacher, they must not let the young, of both sexes, go without instruction in the Torah.
—Ethical Will of Eleazar of Mainz, c. 1357.

Telegrams

Telegrams are dramatic in their effect. The telegram form conveys a sense of immediacy and emergency. It is apt for any content which needs to be made more "current"-feeling, or for that which is already current. Composing a telegram is simple, but students should work from one or two examples. And it is good to discuss how words are counted in a telegram, and how telegraph companies charge by the word. Brevity should become more than mere brevity, it should become the art of concise expression in a good telegram.

Telegrams which might actually be sent include all the categories found under Letters above. In addition, telegrams describing the urgent needs of tzedakah organizations, urgent messages from the past to the future, or urgent messages from the future to the past might be considered.

What telegram would you send to Saul on the eve of his final battle with the Philistines? What telegram would David have sent to him on that occasion? What telegram would Samuel have sent? Or, what telegram would Samuel send to us today, if he could?

Reading, Writing, and Comprehension

The three skills which form the focus of this chapter are among the most essential from a Jewish point of view. Judaism is first and foremost a literary tradition. Jewish heritage is open to all who are literate, and closed to the illiterate. The Torah is read aloud so that even those who cannot themselves read can, in effect, "read" it. It is not only read aloud, but in the tradition of the Scribes, it is also interpreted—reiterated in the plain language of everyday life—so that those who cannot master the language of the Torah will be able to "understand" it.

A Jewish communal worker once asked me, "What is the one thing that, if you could have it, would significantly improve the quality of Jewish education?" Without hesitation, I replied, "Great teachers."

"That's right," he said, "If you have great teachers you don't even need textbooks."

"Wrong," I said. "If you have great teachers, they never do without textbooks. They know how to use them."

Making yourself a master teacher means learning to use textbooks and other written materials effectively. Jewish master teachers have known this for thousands of years. In fact, it was in response to the need for a good textbook that the sages created the Mishnah, and then went on for hundreds of years to develop it further until they had the entire Talmud.

Texts are just one of the tools in the kit of the master teacher. But texts are the hammer. And it is a poor carpenter who refuses to learn how best to use a hammer.

Learning Systems

Some years ago I addressed the faculty and students of a Jewish school of education on the major problems facing all educators. I began by quoting from Arthur Combs' excellent work *Myths of Education*. Combs said,"We have beautiful school buildings, good programs, excellent materials, dedicated teachers, devoted principals. The problem is *the parents send us the wrong children.*"

This is, of course, an exaggeration. Actually, the children who come to us are just right. And their parents bring them to religious school religiously—(which, for many parents—and I say this without criticism—is the only thing they do religiously). The real problem is that all education is experimental.

Every child has a slightly different way of assimilating information—a slightly different learning system. Since no two children are alike, at any age or in any grade, by definition all education is experimental.

Some children learn best when confronted by written materials, or through the act of writing. (Many adults continue, long after their academic careers are essentially over, to swear by the act of taking notes. They write intensely during lectures, take notes on books they read, and use the act of writing as a tool for memory.) Other children learn best through hearing and speaking. Still others learn best through seeing and imagining. And a goodly number operate by "getting a feel" for new material, relying on their tactile and emotional sensibilities for developing a sense of "comfortableness" with what they learn.

Of course, all of us use all of these systems to one degree or another. And no one learns exclusively through one system—that would make teaching too simple. Teaching is complex. It is experimental and laboratory-oriented. The classroom is the teacher's laboratory, and the project is always the same: to turn ordinary lead into gold. Truly, it is a miracle that learning ever happens at all.

One thing we can say for a fact: No one set of techniques is ever enough. The teacher who has mastered the techniques of reading and writing has only begun the work of giving appropriate options for all the learning systems in a classroom.

It took two rabbinic friends—Stuart Kelman and Jack Bloom—to convince me to study the principles and practices of Neurolinguistic Programming (NLP). The best way I can describe NLP is to say that it is a trail guide to more sensitive communication. It has altered the way I see, hear, and feel the world around me. And it has given me a heightened sensitivity to the many learning systems which students use. In practical terms NLP teaches that we must use greater diversity in teaching—employing as many of the senses as possible to motivate activities and explicate materials in the classroom.

If you are interested in reading more about NLP, begin with a book called *Frogs into Princes* by Richard Bandler and John Grinder (Moab, UT: Real People Press, 1979). If you are very fortunate, perhaps you can locate a class with an NLP trainer.

Chapter 9
Oral Work

In this chapter

After those activities which utilize reading and writing, the next most common classroom exercises in the religious school are those which involve oral work. Here are eighteen basic techniques which provide a great degree of flexibility in the use of oral work in teaching.

The Verbal Dimension

The cognitive psychologist David Ausubel has done extensive research on the verbal dimension in teaching. He points out that there are two kinds of learning which commonly take place in a classroom: rote learning and meaningful learning. Many teachers encourage rote learning by requiring students to utilize the teacher's vocabulary and wording in reiterating key concepts. This approach is a trap.

One year, shortly before Ḥanukkah, I had occasion to sit in on a class of fourth graders. The teacher, very much aware of the presence of an observer in her classroom, decided to show off what the students had learned concerning the upcoming holiday. In rapid-fire sequence, she conducted an oral review of the material she had taught. She asked short-answer questions like "How many sons did Mattathias have?" "How many candles are on the Ḥanukkah menorah?" "What was the motto of the Maccabees?" "Against what army did the Maccabees fight?" "What were the Maccabees fighting for?"

The answers showed that the students had been well-prepared for any type of testing. What intrigued me most was the answer to the last question, "What were the Maccabees fighting for?," as one little nine-year-old girl said, "For religious freedom."

Shortly thereafter I left the classroom and waited in the hall. When the nine-year-old girl emerged from class, I stopped her and asked, "What is religious freedom?" She answered, "That's what the Maccabees were fighting for."

This is a good example of the trap of rote learning. The student had learned something, all right. She had learned a tautology: "What were the Maccabees fighting for?" "Religious freedom." "What is religious freedom?" "What the

In the second stage the learner consciously acts upon [a] concept or proposition [learned either through discovery or simple reception] in an attempt to remember it so that it will be available at some future time. He may do this in either of two distinct ways. If the learner attempts to retain the idea by relating it to what he knows, and thereby "make sense" out of it, then *meaningful learning* will result, On the other hand, if the learner merely attempts to memorize the idea, without relating it to his existing knowledge, then *rote learning* is said to take place.
—David P. Ausubel, and Floyd G. Robinson, *School Learning: An Introduction to Educational Psychology* (New York: Holt, Rinehart and Winston, Inc., 1969).

Maccabees were fighting for." This kind of circular learning is very satisfying to the teacher who scores a perfect answer for the child on an examination featuring short-answer or true/false questions. It does not make for meaningful learning.

In order for information to be useful, the learner must be equipped to act upon the information in some way. If the learner merely memorizes new information without making it a part of a larger cognitive structure, this is rote learning. Meaningful learning only occurs when the learner attempts to relate new information to information and data already known—that is, to make the information a part of his or her everyday world.

The best way to avoid rote learning and encourage meaningful learning is to listen to students—to encourage verbal activities in which students must rephrase, in their own words, the meaning of what has been learned. If the teacher had spent time doing this with her fourth graders, the nine-year-old girl might have been able to connect the idea of religious freedom to her everyday world. She might have first thought of the meaning of freedom, then the meaning of religion, then learned to bring these two together to make a concept that was not only what the Maccabees fought for, but something really worth fighting for—then and now.

All activities employing verbal skills, when used by the master teacher, have this in common: they encourage meaningful learning.

Verbal Activities

Reports on reading

Naturally, the first dimension in oral activities concerns the reiteration and rephrasing of what has been read or written. The usual way in which verbal reports on reading are given is for one student to speak while all the others in the classroom listen. This method has the advantage of helping students develop good speaking and listening skills and habits. It has sever disadvantages, however.

It forces students to place themselves in the risky position of being open to criticism from their peers, if not from the teacher. And it forces many students to sit quietly while one student recites— a situation which leads to classroom discipline problems.

It should be made clear at the outset that the reception/discovery and meaningful/rote dimensions *do not* describe simple dichotomies, but instead are more in the nature of continua. For example, insofar as educational settings are concerned, one rarely finds a pure discovery approach, but rather, varying degrees of "guided" discovery. Similarly, on the other dimension, the meaningfulness or roteness of the learning depends on a number of factors, some of which are variable quantities. Consequently, although we may abridge our description for convenience, any learning that occurs is not simply either meaningful or rote; it is, instead, *more or less* meaningful or *more or less* rote.

—Ausubel and Robinson, *School Learning: An Introduction to Educational Psychology.*

You may wish to consider some alternatives to this procedure. One is to use small groups as the sounding boards for student reports. While other groups are working in learning centers, or doing written work, a group of five or six students can work together giving oral reports to one another, with the teacher listening in. In this way, the process becomes less threatening, and discipline becomes less of a potential problem.

Alternatively, oral reports can be presented in panel discussions which group sets of related reading material together. In this way, five or six of the class members work together to create a series of short oral reports which reinforce one another. While it is true that this is still a format in which one student speaks while the rest of the class listens, the panel discussion approach means that a goodly percentage of the students in the class are taking part in "the presentation" and have a vested interest in listening. This also increases the odds that other students will remain attentive.

Descriptions of photographs, maps, models, or charts

Oral work which requires students to paraphrase what they have learned through the description of objects and other visual aids—photographs, maps, models, charts, etc.—also puts students into the position of drawing upon their knowledge of the way the world is to incorporate and make meaningful new concepts and ideas.

Teachers often decorate rooms with elaborate bulletin boards and posters for new units, but sometimes forget to make use of these decorations for their obvious purpose—to help students gain a complete awareness of a new topic. By asking individual students to describe portions of the decorations and objects in the classroom, the teacher can utilize such displays most effectively.

Another visual area in which teachers sometimes fall short is in the use of photographs, maps, charts, and other visual dimensions of textbooks. A study conducted some years ago by the National Education Association proved that the most widely read materials in any textbook are the captions that accompany the illustrations. This seems natural. After all, the eye is first drawn to illustrations, and only secondarily to text. It is equally natural to suggest that teachers might wish to consider "teaching" the illustrations as well as the text. And one very effective way of teaching the illustrations is through asking students to look at an

Seven Guidelines for Bulletin Boards:

1. Think little. Don't try to cover too many different subjects at one time. You don't have the space, and you don't want one subject to compete with (and distract from) another.
2. Think big. Grab attention with big headlines and big pictures which may be easily seen from the distance.
3. Think simple. Don't confuse. Don't be too complicated.
4. Think bright. Use bright colors, bright words, and bright illustrations.
5. Think "now." Be timely. What is happening this week (or next week) is usually more relevant than what will happen three months from now.
6. Think broadly. A bulletin board is for more than just bulletins. It is also a show place for exhibiting posters, art work, etc.
7. Think who. Your bulletin board need not be a do-it-yourself project. Make it a class project.

—Carol Tauben, and Edith Abrahams, *Integrating Arts and Crafts in the Jewish School: A Step by Step Guide.*

illustration together while one student describes it. This activity avoids the doldrums sometimes accompanying individual recitation since every student has reason to focus personally on what is being described in order to determine the accuracy of the description.

Using new vocabulary

It is common for language teachers to utilize activities which encourage students to make use of new vocabulary. It is equally important for the teacher of Judaica. As in the little Ḥanukkah story I told above, this is an excellent way of determining that meaningful learning has taken place.

Students can be asked to make sentences using the new vocabulary, and encouraged to make these sentences in such a way that the sentences incorporate the new learning in the framework of the students' everyday world.

Alternatively, students can be asked to interact with one another in small groups or in pairs building oral sentences and checking them with one another. In teaching a subject such as conversational Hebrew this, of course, becomes one of the basic building blocks of learning. It is equally effective in teaching ritual, history, Jewish law, and many other subjects.

Also, running verbally throuyh a glossary of new terms is an effective way of reviewing new learning together as a group.

Questions and Answers

Ask questions during the course of instruction about each point that is important for students to master, rather than depend upon a general, indirect consequence from questioning.—"On Asking People Questions" by R.C. Anderson and W. B. Biddle in G. H. Bower, ed., *The Psychology of Learning and Motivation* (New York: Academic Press, 1975).

The Ḥanukkah story above also provides an example of using short question-and-answer sessions as a mode for quick review. Provided that the teacher does not overly stress the need for students to reiterate in the teacher's precise words the answers to these questions, but encourages the students to answer in their own words, this can be another quick path to meaningful learning.

With a little effort and creativity, this kind of oral review can be made into a game by dividing the students into evenly-balanced teams and giving points for answers.

Round-table discussion

A verbal activity can also be planned directly as a round-table discussion. The students can be the panelists, and the discussion can be centered around the concepts studied in a text or other reading materials. With a little planning, several round tables can go on at one and the same time—allowing all students in the class to be involved in oral activity simultaneously.

A little more planning may make it possible—when studying history, for example—for students not only to participate in a round table, but also to play roles as famous people, using their imaginations to make oral presentations as these people might have made them in a similar round-table discussion.

Committee reports

Leaving behind the individual oral presentation, the committee report makes an excellent forum for oral activity. It is good motivationally because it is strong on both activity and socialization. It encourages written, as well as verbal, comprehension skills. Committee reports teach cooperation, listening, and speaking. The preparation time can be given in class, or committees can be required, where possible, to meet outside class in order to prepare.

Tape recording

The advent of portable cassette tape and video recorders has opened a whole new dimension in classroom teaching. Tapes can be made in advance and played back or screened for the class. The tapes can then be incorporated by the teacher into the total learning environment—used at the appropriate moments in order to drive home a concept or idea, or used as a form of review.

Telephone dialogues

Especially in Hebrew teaching, telephone dialogues can be an interesting alternative to merely speaking in class. If you are of a dramatic bent, you can import toy telephones into the class to enhance the realistic effect.

Students have a tendency to feel comfortable in the use of the telephone and to extend this comfort to the use of even a toy telephone in the classroom. This also brings a dimension of the everyday world into the classroom.

But you don't have to be teaching language to use the telephone dialogue technique. You only have to pose a simple query in terms of the telephone. If Deborah could have called Samuel, what might they have had to say to one another? If an Eastern European Jew from the shtetl could talk to a Western European Jew from the ghetto, what might they have had to say to one another? If a Sephardic Jew from the mellah could have had a conversation with an Ashkenazic Jew in Detroit in the 1900's, what would they have learned about their respective worlds? If Purim could

Akiba on the Telephone

"Phoning" a friend to use verbal behavior in the classroom can be used in classes teaching rabbinics, history, and other subjects, too. In the midst of other forms of questioning, you can ask a student sitting in one part of the room to spontaneously have a telephone conversation with a student in another part of the room. But ask the second student to be Akiba or Beruriah, or whomever you are studying.

In younger grades—and even at times with adults—you can ask the second person to be an inanimate object such as the tablets of the Ten Commandments, the First Temple, or the Eternal Light.

call up Pesaḥ, what might they talk about? If Thanksgiving could have a phone conversation with Sukkot, what would they say? And so on.

Tell a story

Students do not have to limit their verbal activities to reportage. One of the world's most fascinating phenomena is the ability people have to concoct stories extemporaneously and to retell stories they have heard. There is no grade level on which this ability cannot be tapped. Even the youngest children delight in retelling a simple story or in telling personal stories about themselves and about their families.

Stories which students learn can also be among the most valuable forms of learning. The student who understands the meaning of a story often understands a subject more deeply than he or she might in any other fashion. Students demonstrate the depth of their understanding through telling and retelling stories.

And while we are speaking of stories—and the use of stories in the classroom—it is important to know a few salient facts about how teachers can best use stories. First, by telling them. Students do not mind even if the teacher reads a story aloud from a book or from an index card or sheet of paper. What is important is that a story is a part of the teacher's toolkit, and the master teacher uses stories all the time.

Second, students—especially young children, but actually all students—love to hear a good story more than once. And all of us love to hear the same story told in many different ways. So, don't be afraid to tell a story over and over until the students can reiterate it and rephrase it for themslves. And encourage students to retell the stories which you tell to them in class at home to their parents. In many ways, the bulk of all Jewish learning is either packaged as stories or ready to be used in story form.

Third, stories are available in many different forms. The most important ones are often available as books, on film, on records, on cassette tape, or on videotape. Students will appreciate them in more than one form.

Relate historical to current events

What makes the study of anything historical relevant to us is our ability to hear echoes of the past in the present. Young students have less appreciation of this fact than their elders, since, as Aḥad Haam succinctly pointed out, they have less past to recall. Nevertheless, they are well-versed in the

What Makes a Good Story?

1. Plot, conflict, and suspense.
2. Quick action: something must happen all the time.
3. Simple elements that are either familiar to the students or similar to familiar ones, without being humdrum.
4. Emotional coloring.
5. Universal appeal.
6. Repetition.
7. Some situation revealed by the storyteller to the listener, of which the character in the story is quite ignorant.
—adapted from "Suggestions on Storytelling" by Lillie Rubee in Lawrence Meyers, *Teaching in the Jewish Religious School.*

present, and so they are well-equipped to assimilate the past as a form of learning, and not only as a form of direct experience. Else there would be no human interest in history.

What this means in the end is that all history is your history. All you have to do is to reach out and relate it to yourself. Doing so is an excellent exercise for the verbal skills. It is very much like telling a story, the only difference being that these stories connect you to the past. "Can you think of a time when something like this happened to you?" is a key question. "Does this remind you of anything that you know?" is another. There are about a dozen more. They all have the same point: To make what is historical into what is relevant.

Round-robin

The round-robin is an oral activity which involves the whole class and takes very little time. The teacher poses a question of opinion or value, and then allows each student a one-sentence answer. Students can be asked to respond in class seating-order or at random, but the method works best when every student has a chance to either answer or say "Pass." This technique is as good in Hebrew teaching as in the teaching of Judaica, so long as the questions or issues posed call for short answers.

Conversation

Among the oral exercises are interactive forms. The teacher can converse with one pupil, allowing the class to act as "listeners." Or, two pupils can converse with one another while the teacher and class act as listeners. What is alluring about this particular method of oral work is that simple conversation is a comfortable form for most students, and so the activity can be used at almost any age level with good results. It is also among the best of the impromptu forms of oral activity.

Interview

The interview is an interesting form of interactive oral work. Commonly, one student prepares by studying an historical figure, a place, a time, a custom, etc., and is then interviewed by the remainder of the class. The prepared pupil becomes the teacher in an active sense.

A group of pupils can prepare themselves to be interviewed in the same way. And, alternatively, the teacher can be interviewed, as well. Many creative teachers find it useful to pose as an historical figure, a holiday, a law, an

Abraham Joshua Heschel reminds us that, although we pray together as a congregation, prayers are always offered up in the heart of an individual. The sermon is a way of allowing students self-expression. It is, by its very nature, an oral activity. And yet it goes beyond most of the oral activities mentioned in chapter eight. Specifically, it is the expression of an individual.

In his excellent book called *Jewish Prayer*, Louis Jacobs quotes a tombstone found in an English village that conveys (in a somewhat ironic manner) what may be the ultimate sermon:

Here lies Martin Elbingrod,
  Have mercy on my soul,
  Lord God.
As I would do were I Lord God,
  And you were Martin Elbingrod.

You might also consider asking pupils to be their own parents, to be the rabbi, or even to be the author of your textbook!

An instructive incident can be related in this regard: A student in one of my classes was stuck for the answer to a particularly thorny question. I merely suggested that she pretend to be the author of the textbook, and the answer was immediately quite apparent and available to her. It was a mental trick, borrowed from Neurolinguistic Programming, but it worked.

object, etc., and allow the class to become verbally interactive as students try either to guess who or what the teacher is or the identity of the teacher's *persona*.

Panel of "experts"—seated committee reports

A similar approach is taken through the use of seated committee reports, where students on the committee prepare themselves to respond to questions as a panel of experts. This form of oral activity is very much in line with the whole issue of meaningful learning. It is impossible for students to "fake" an understanding in responding in this fashion. The understanding is either there or it is obviously missing. In either case, it makes for an opportunity to further the work of the classroom through oral interaction.

Debate

Closely related to other forms of small-group and committee interactive oral exercises is the debate. Almost any subject lends itself to the debate format, so long as the teacher can state a problem in the classical debate form—Resolved: Since "Condition A" then "Result B." For example, "Resolved: That since the British have offered the Jewish people the land of Uganda, the Jewish people agree to make Uganda their homeland." Or "Resolved: That since Jewry is under attack in the Soviet Union only as a religion, the Jews in the Soviet Union should give up any practice of Judaism."

The teacher should beware of assigning debates in the form of questions, or without a formal statement such as one of the above. Debates become conversations when they are phrased as questions, and they tend to become one-sided when not phrased as controversial statements. Remember—it is not important which side "wins" a debate provided that the issues are spelled out in such a way that any discussion which follows can utilize them as a starting point.

Also, one of the arts of debating is that both teams are encouraged to prepare both sides, thus learning the strengths and weaknesses of arguments on both sides of a question. It is only at the final moment before debating that a team is told which side it will represent. This decision can be made by the teacher, or can depend on the flip of a coin, etc.

Students who are asked to prepare a debate will need time for preparation, even if the debate is a culmination of what has been taught. They also may need some guidance in finding the most appropriate arguments for each side of the debate. It is therefore often appropriate to invite a second "teacher" (an assistant or a parent) into the classroom to work with one of the two sides while the teacher works with the other.

Citation

As students prepare debates they learn how to seek out relevant citations from textual materials as "evidence." The class text can be used for this purpose, and other textbooks on the same subject, or ancillary materials on the same subject, may also be used as sources. Typically, sources are grouped into pro and con materials, as well.

This leads to an independent oral technique which consists entirely of locating the most appropriate citation for a statement. In this activity, the teacher prepares a series of statements, each of which can be verified in fact by a citation from the text. Students are asked to search out the proper quotation in support or contradiction of the teacher's statements in the class text or other sources, and then to read the citation aloud.

With a little imagination, this can be turned into a game with teams and points. It makes an excellent rapid review technique for homework assignments that consist of reading.

Town meeting

The furthest extension of interactive oral work is the "town meeting." This activity makes it possible for the entire class to participate verbally at one and the same time. The teacher or a prepared student can raise issues as if the class were a town or a council sitting in a particular imaginary time and place.

The students must, of course, be prepared for this activity by first learning as much as possible about the mind-set of people in the place and time they are to represent. Beyond this, they can apply the force of their own personalities to the exercise, giving themselves the opportunity of internalizing new learnings in a very active, social, and comfortable manner. This activity incorporates all the necessities for perfect motivation.

A number of the oral techniques reviewed in this chapter are really a part of that textbook on teaching textbooks that I meant to write. This method of asking students to cite quotations from their textbook encourages the students to view the textbook as a valuable aid and resource. It also encourages students to open their textbooks outside of class, since it points up the relevance of the text to the course of study.

Group-think

Group-think is a good technique for introducing a new unit or starting a new lesson using oral activity. The teacher asks what students think of a particular subject, know about a particular subject, or feel about a particular subject. The class responds by giving single words or brief answers that the teacher can then record on the chalkboard. The list of words which is compiled can serve as a starting point from which the lesson can be launched. Teachers can also feel free to add a few words of their own. If students offer lengthy verbal responses, it becomes the teacher's chore to pare them down to a word or two that will fit with the other words listed.

This is a very common technique which almost every teacher has either used or experienced in the classroom, but it bears mention precisely for this reason.

Oral interaction in the classroom

There is no way that one can teach without some form of oral interaction. Even if the student's response is mere silence, communication requires the transmission of speech. In earlier times, Jewish students were made to memorize and recite by memory long stretches of text. Even earlier, before formal texts were in common use, students prepared themslevs to be teachers by learning by rote the exact words and configurations of words which their teachers used. This led the sages to opine that there were four types of students: the sponge, the funnel, the strainer, and the sieve:

> a sponge soaks up everything; a funnel lets in at one end and out at the other; a strainer lets the wine pass through and retains the dregs;]and[a sieve lets out the coarse and retains the fine flour. (*Avot* 5:18)

You might think that it is best to have a memory like a sponge—to soak up everything. Actually, each of the four kinds of student helps to maintain Judaism in a different way.

The sponge is the student who has what we call a "photographic" memory. This kind of student remembers everything learned, precisely as it is learned. The problem with this kind of study is that it is rote, and, as we have seen, the rote memorization of what is studied is only the beginning of learning.

What is meant by the funnel is a little deceptive. At first you may think that it means a student who forgets the learning as soon as the test has been taken. But there is another possibility. Just as a funnel is wider on one end and more narrow at the other, the sages may have referred to a student who can reduce knowledge to a bare minimum. This student condenses and summ. izes in an efficient manner everything which has been stud. ¹. In academic terms, such students are sometimes referrea .o as "popularizers," and the work they do in digesting materials makes the materials more easily accessble to others.

The strainer is the least likely to be important, yet even the strainer has an advantage. While other students remember the most important parts of a teaching, the strainer is capable of retaining impurities, and often these have proven very important in the end. It is for this reason that the Talmud, for example, not only includes the decisions and important arguments of the victors in each discussion, but the positions of the losers, as well. Even these arguments bear repetition, if only to reassure us that the better argument won.

The sieve student is more precise. This student knows the difference between what is important and what is not. He or she does not merely "clump" materials to make them more concrete, but also separates the materials into classes of importance, dealing with the important ones and holding the minor ones in abeyance.

All of the various kinds of students can sharpen their wits on oral exercises. But what is even more important is that through the use of oral activities, the teacher can come to identify the kinds of students in the classroom and begin to know their learning styles more intimately. This, in turn, can make the teacher more effective in teaching. The master teacher learns the students' learning styles and uses them individually, giving each student the kind of attention—and amount of attention—which is necessary to bring about meaningful learning.

Chapter 10
Drama in the Classroom

In this chapter

Drama is creative experience. It elicits emotion. It releases the author, director, actor, and audience in us. It facilitates what Buber called "the instinct to origination" (see Chapter 4). The dramatic techniques below, divided into four main categories and twenty or so activity types, are classroom-oriented, and are intended to be incorporated in teaching rather than as a curriculum for drama itself.

The Value of Classroom Drama

Drama enhances identification. Through drama, students identify with roles outside their normal experience. They assume characters. They interact with other assumed characters. Dramatic techniques lift learning from its accustomed mode of analysis to a real experience.

Drama also motivates data-gathering—by depicting events, characters, and scenes, students learn details of customs, dress, feelings, situations, occupations and speech.

On a mundane level, drama enhances verbalization and personai communication. On a deeper level, drama embeds learning in the *skills memory* (see Chapter 15) of the student. Once in skills memory, learning tends to be long-term as opposed to short-term. Drama promotes meaningful rather than rote learning.

Drama enhances group cohesiveness through its emphasis on cooperation. As Buber observed, education enables us to share our instinct to origination with others. Some educational philosophers call this function "socialization." Especially in the diaspora, the need to meld individuals into a community makes Jewish education indispensable for our survival. Drama can be a strong tool for forging unity.

There is, of course, one caveat: The potential that drama possesses for enhancing awareness is also drama's greatest danger. It is important to utilize drama with respect, taking care not to overstep boundaries of good taste and borders of sensitivity. Some naturally dramatic subjects should not be dramatized in the classroom. As teachers, we may not be equipped to deal with the emotional reactions which highly emotionally-charged drama may unleash.

For example, life-threatening or fear-provoking situations drawn from the Holocaust are often beyond the realm of good taste. In fact, they may actually prove harmful even to students who do not appear overly sensitive on the surface. This danger is *prima facie* evidence of the very real power of classroom drama.

Dramatic Techniques

Below are a few techniques in classroom drama. The list is not comprehensive. There are many excellent books on drama on the market and some include classroom suggestions.

For our purposes, dramatic techniques can be divided into four main categories: (a) associative drama—indirect dramatic exercises and activities; (b) extemporaneous drama—simple and impromptu dramatic exercises which directly involve individual students or small groups of students; (c) formal drama—plays, pageants, and the like— which are formally rehearsed and presented; and (d) alternative forms—techniques which fall outside the formal and informal patterns.

Associative Drama

The term "associative drama" encompasses dramatic techniques in which learners participate in the third person (so to speak)—by association, and not directly. Associative drama provides non-threatening ways of introducing dramatics to the classroom. Students are not "exposed" before their peers, as they might be in role-plays and staged dramas. Nevertheless, associative drama may be very powerful. And it has numerous applications, especially in set induction.

Just how powerful associative drama can be was made clear to me in a workshop given many years ago by Joyce Klein, a gifted Jewish dramatic educator. Although I may have modified her technique slightly over the years, I still refer to it as the "Klein circle."

The Elements of Classroom Drama

All classroom drama requires at least six elements.

The teacher must

1. The teacher must set the mood for the drama, play, or story to be enacted.
2. The teacher must create an environment in which the dramatic activity is appropriate.
3. The teacher must present the material from which the drama can evolve.
4. The teacher must discuss the plan of action or the method of the drama with the students.
5. The teacher must guide students to enter into the drama with understanding and belief.
6. The teacher must help students to evaluate the meaning of the dramatic activity once it is complete.

Failures in the use of drama in the classroom can usually be traced to the omission or inadequacy of one of these elements.

The Klein Circle

Draw a circle on the chalkboard. Tell the class that the circle represents a person, and ask them to "fill in" facial features. With early learners (through grade four or five), you can give the children the chalk (provided you have drawn the circle low enough for them to easily reach it) as they suggest adding eyes, ears, hair, and so on. Otherwise, the teacher can add the facial features. At some point, ask the class to decide, either by consensus or hand vote, the sex and age of the person being drawn. There is seldom a need for the teacher to control what sex or age the class determines.

After all the facial features have been added, ask the class to give the figure a name—preferably a Jewish name. The circle is now a "person" with an "identity."

This is the time to lay down the only "rules" of this game. Specify a time and place or a situation in which the chalkboard figure is enmeshed. For example, if the students have chosen to draw a female aged twelve named Rachel, you could say something like, "This is as much as I will tell you: Rachel is living in Spain in the year 1492. Her family is packing all their belongings. They have been Marranos for many years and tomorrow they must leave their home forever."

Next, ask students to specify the proper emotional atmosphere. How does Rachel feel today? Ask the class to probe their personal experiences of moving or leaving home. They may say that Rachel is "excited," "scared," "worried," "hurried," and so on. As they suggest emotions and attitudes, record their answers on the chalkboard around the figure.

You are now ready to enter a teaching mode. If this is the beginning of a unit, ask the students to imagine what will happen to Rachel in the next few hours, days, weeks, months, and years of her life. If this is the end of a unit, ask students to open their texts and cite sentences and paragraphs that give clues as to what is about to happen to Rachel.

You will soon build a collective "biography" for Rachel. The biography will include many of the details of what is to be learned in the unit, or many of the details of what has already been learned in the unit.

As the chalkboard simulation progresses, it is easy to add additional circles to represent members of Rachel's family, or friends and neighbors. You will be able to build characters and biographies for each of them in the same way. It is also quite natural at some point to invite members of the class to take the parts of Rachel and her family and friends. In this way, associative drama can blend into role-playing.

This elegant technique operates in many dimensions. It introduces drama to the classroom without requiring students to perform in front of their peers. Yet students find themselves motivated by and involved in the process because the characters are ones they have "created" together. This makes it easy for students to identify with the characters.

The Flannelgraph

A second form of associative drama is the flannel board, sometimes called the "flannelgraph." Before the advent of Velcro, there was flannel. It was discovered that flannel adheres to flannel by means of static electricity. The flannelgraph is merely a piece of flannel material stretched on a frame or mounted on a board of plywood. Figures cut out of flannel and placed on the flannelgraph represent elements of background (for example, trees, wells, hills, clouds, etc.) or characters or objects in a particular story or play.

In early grades, stories can be illustrated by the teacher through the manipulation of the flannel characters and objects on the flannelgraph. Very young students can be encouraged to imaginatively manipulate figures, objects, and backgrounds on the flannelgraph during free play. This kind of activity is also appropriate for older children, but older children are less likely to take advantage of imaginative play opportunities.

With older children, the flannelgraph is best used as a tool for associative role-play. Individual students can be asked to manipulate characters and objects and backgrounds in recreating an historical situation or in retelling a story or in completing a review for a unit of study about a significant individual or group.

The flannelgraph, like the Klein circle, does not force the student to use gross motor skills or to be exposed to peer critique as in direct role-play or formal drama.

The Puppet Box

The flannelgraph and the Klein circle share severe limitations in terms of flexibility. Puppets, on the other hand, begin in associative forms of drama and naturally extend outward to the most sophisticated and ritualized formal drama. You can use finger puppets, hand puppets, body puppets, stick

The technique represented by the blackboard circle takes into cognizance all of the elements for good classroom drama, even though it is drama only at its simplest level. Be certain, however, that you pause to evaluate the meaning of the activity once it is complete. In drama, as in all forms of classroom learning, closure is a *sine qua non.*

puppets, marionettes, or any other of the many permutations of what we call puppets. To one degree or another, all of these shield the puppeteer from his or her audience.

In younger grades, you may wish to keep a box of puppets (just as you may keep a "dress-up" box) in the classroom. The puppet box should hold homemade or store-bought puppets. It may also be used to contain basic materials for creating new puppets. When a story is particularly interesting, or when a situation in history is intrinsically intriguing, reach for the puppet box. Remove the puppets one at a time and display them to the class. Can these be used for the characters you need in the situations you wish to recreate? What kinds of simple costuming might be added? Do the students wish to make new puppets to go with the telling? Should new creations be hand puppets made from stockings and cardboard? What should the characters look like? What materials need to be added? All these considerations make for excellent review and summary of a lesson, even as they prepare the class for an activity.

When the puppets are ready, assign one to each student. Let the students manipulate the puppets to act out the roles. Teach them to use a free hand and arm as a miniature stage. And allow all the students to try on at least one puppet.

Students in older grades do not always like using their arms as stages. For older students and adults, you may also wish to have an old refrigerator or washing machine carton cut to make a stage.

Last but not least, if a successful drama is created through the use of puppets, consider the possibility of inviting another class or a group of parents to see it played out. This can be a very effective culmination of puppetry activities.

Extemporaneous Drama

Closely allied to associative drama are the many forms of extemporaneous or unrehearsed drama. The two types of dramatic activity blend in actual use, and we separate them here only for purposes of simplification. As with associative drama, this list is not comprehensive.

In college, I majored in drama for a year. I was interested in dramatic writing and stage lighting, particularly. Like most of your students, I was shy of the stage itself, afraid to be an "actor." Nevertheless, and despite being

There is no particularly appropriate time for extemporaneous drama to take place. Or, to phrase this in another way, every moment is a good moment for extemporaneous drama. For the teacher who is truly alert in the classroom, opportunities for using extemporaneous drama abound. You merely have to look at what is happening—in the course, in the classroom, in the text, in current events, and in the life of the school—to find your subject matter.

stage-shy, I found myself drawn into the spirit of extemporaneous drama because it was so difficult to err. The worst I could do was to look preposterous; and even the best actors in the class often looked preposterous in extemporaneous roles. No one had an edge.

This element of equality makes extemporaneous drama a useful classroom tool. Even shy students find themselves able to respond to psychodramas and sociodramas, provided these are introduced in a nonthreatening atmosphere. The key to creating this atmosphere is humor. As long as you maintain your sense of humor, and allow humor to be a part of the dramatic process, any of the techniques below will work like a charm.

Charades

Nearly everyone is familiar with charades, and you can use this familiarity as an entree to the world of extemporaneous drama. Charades are also valuable in teaching Hebrew or Hebrew terms, since the game is basically vocabulary drill.

Use charades to review lists of words or important phrases; to have students illustrate in action the meaning of words or phrases; and to provide relief from intensely text-oriented or intellectual exercises.

"Psychodramas" or "Sociodramas"

Very often the two terms "psychodrama" and "sociodrama" are used interchangeably. There is no reason not to use them this way. However, I like to distinguish them. The psychodrama, in my parlance, is an extemporaneous monologue, while the sociodrama is an extemporaneous play in which characters interact. Both forms are very effective in the classroom; both require careful, but not overly difficult, preparation on the part of the instructor.

Psychodrama: To prepare a psychodrama, identify an historical individual or an anonymous individual in a historical setting or a critical situation. Write a scenario (try to keep it brief) suggesting the situation and the attitudes and emotions that might inhabit the individual in such a situation. For example:

> *Queen Esther*
> *You are Queen Esther. You have not told King Ahasuerus that you are Jewish. Now Haman is planning to murder all the Jews. Mordekhai, your uncle, says you must do something to stop Haman. He says, "Who knows? Maybe you have been made Queen just so that you can help your*

people!" But you know how dangerous it is. First, the King ordered you not to come to him unless he calls. If you appear before him, he can either (a) welcome you by raising his golden scepter in your direction, or (b) have you killed for disobeying his orders. And, second, if you fail, the King and Haman will know you are a Jew and you will be murdered along with all the other Jews of Persia. Think about how you would feel if you were really Queen Esther and talk to us about your problem until you come to a decision—your own decision.

Give this brief scenario to one of the students in the class and ask the student to work out the problem as a monologue, letting the class in on the thought processes employed.

Sociodrama: The sociodrama is an extension of the psychodrama. Here you write out several roles and ask the students to interact, using their own perceptions of each role. To the role of Queen Esther in the example above, you might add the roles of Haman and King Ahasuerus. And you might suggest to each of the three players that the scene take place at the banquet given by Esther for the King and Haman.

The outline for the story comes from the Book of Esther itself, and is not difficult to prepare. Students can easily identify with the characters and the situation.

Reenacting critical situations—a form of sociodrama

If you are studying historical situations, the sociodrama can be extended to anonymous characters caught in the web of history. For example, you might ask one student to portray a young Zionist in Russia who wants to go to Israel (as a part of the First Aliyah). The student's predicament is to go home to a father and a mother (portrayed by two other students) and explain why it is necessary to leave family and friends behind and to go to Palestine (a barren and primitive land) to build a new nation for Jews.

Simulation games

Building outward from sociodrama is simulation gaming. The simulation game is typically a carefully orchestrated and prepared form of extemporaneous drama. It often involves the entire class in a series of roles. Roles can be identified by groups, or individual roles can be assigned. Usually the steps

There are many who claim that Jewish life is a series of "crises." Rawidowicz once penned an intriguing essay called "Israel: The Ever-Dying People" in which he argues that this particularly Jewish attitude of considering ourselves ever in danger of disappearing is actually a way we have of insuring our very survival.

In a sense, we tend to turn to religion especially in moments of tension and distress. This is also useful. Transforming a critical moment into a simple classroom drama can help students cope with the moment, and can also be instructive in teaching students to let out their personal concerns. Since we all "read ourselves into" critical moments— asking how we would feel in a particular situation, and how we would react—it is also a powerful psychological and sociological tool for teachers.

to be followed are outlined for each role. Good examples of simulation games can be found in the catalogues of several major Jewish publishers. Some years back I was involved in the editing of two of the most ambitious Jewish simulation games. One was by Marcia and Alvan Kaunfer and was called *Dilemma!*; the other was *Exodus—The Russian Jewry Simulation Game* by Elissa Blaser. Describing them will give you some idea of the nature of a simulation game.

In *Dilemma!* the class or group played the part of a Federation faced with requests for funds from many worthy causes. Each group of students was assigned a cause to sponsor and given background material on the cause. Causes included a Jewish family service, Israel, a Jewish hospital, a Jewish home for the aged, and so on. In the first round of play, the students examined the budget requests for their groups' causes and studied why each budget line was essential. In the second round of play, the students met together as a group (the "Federation") and listened to each other present impassioned pleas on behalf of the individual causes. In this round of play, the students "discovered" the dilemma. The total amount of the requests exceeded the available funds of the Federation. In the third round, the students went back to their small groups and tried to pare their budgets in some intelligent fashion. In the fourth round, new and smaller budgets were presented, and the group voted on the amounts to be allocated to each of the causes. The game was designed to be played for many hours, even for multiple classroom sessions. Learnings included how federations budget, what kinds of causes federations support, and so on.

Exodus—The Russian Jewry Simulation Game was considerably less extensive. It was designed for play in a single session or "round." And it was designed to mirror the problems a Russian Jew might encounter after deciding to emigrate to Israel. Tables were set up in the classroom to serve as "stations." One station was a bank, another was the KGB office, another was the Office of Emigration, another was a Jewish aid organization, and so on. Each person in the class was assigned a role. Those who were assigned the "stations" as roles were given brief biographies. The KGB person was instructed to be mean to those who came to the "KGB office," the bank teller was instructed to be formal and officious, the Jewish aid person was instructed to be cordial and friendly, and so on. Each was given a list with instructions for each person who would approach them. All the other participants were given roles as Russian Jews. The roles were actual thumbnail biographies of Refuseniks taken from the records of a Russian Jewry organization here in the United States. Each was also numbered. And each was given a "starting point," a first station to approach. A player went to his or her initial station and gave his or her (assumed) name and the key number assigned to it. The station players consulted their lists and told the "Russian Jew" what to do next. For example, the Office of Emigration informed some of the Russian Jews that their visa applications had been "unfortunately misplaced" and they would have to fill out new visa applications. Other Jews were told that their visas had been denied and they would have to seek permission from the KGB office to emigrate. Still others were told that they could only emigrate if they had relatives in Israel. They would have to see the Jewish aid people to see if they had "relatives." (Of course, the Jewish aid people provided such documentation without any problem.) And so on. In the course of play, the game was designed so that only about ten percent of those who applied for visas and had money in the bank could actually emigrate from Russia. Learnings included the frustration of dealing with a highly bureaucratic system, the problems of anti-Semitism in the Soviet Union, and so on. Typically, the game was played for one or two hours, followed by a discussion of the learnings.

You could prepare simulation games on almost any historical situation or critical issue. For example, you could prepare a simple simulation game on the Exodus from Egypt, the Sanhedrin, the options available to Jews just before the destruction of the Second Temple, and so on. Of the forms of extemporaneous drama, the simulation game is the one which requires the most forethought and preparation. But it is the most effective, too. It can involve the entire class at one and the same time; and it places people in realistic situations which involve them deeply and personally. There are whole books devoted to strategies for simulation gaming.

Impromptus

Impromptu drama is an extension of extemporaneous drama. However, the impromptu is usually created by the participants rather than pre-programmed by the teacher.

Impromptu plays: A good example of a technique incorporating impromptu plays is paper bag dramatics. The class is divided into groups and each group is given a paper bag filled with miscellaneous small objects. The groups are required to prepare a skit using all of the objects in their

All of us, whether we are aware of it or not, whether we wish it or not, live in relation to myths. In the past, the myths our people lived by were largely religious and literary—myths of Christian love, of family, of conquest, of bravery in combat...People, one imagines, have never—or have very, very rarely—done arduous things (such as living) just for the thing itself; and the same is no less true today.

There is a difference nowadays, though, or so it seems to me. First, the myths we Americans have lived by are not working ... and we have no new myths to put in their place. The second difference is that the source of mythmaking in our society has changed ... Increasingly, the sources of our myths are movies, journalism, and, most pervasive of all, television. "A Few Sensible Words About Children's TV" —by Michael J. Arlen in *McCall's*, February 1971.

paper bag, based on some theme or incident which is being studied by the class. Sometimes, the groups are all given identical small objects; and sometimes the groups are given paper bags filled with different objects. Objects may include mundane items such as rubber bands, paper clips, pencils, paper, etc. Or they may be more specific items such as kiddush cups, rubber chickens, maps, documents, etc. The assignment may be just for fun, or for learning. For example, after a unit on kibbutz, the groups may be instructed to do plays on kibbutz using paper, pencils, maps of typical kibbutzim, laundry tickets, and so on. The rest is up to the imagination (and humor) of the students.

Television simulations/games: Another whole class of impromptus are games and dramas based on television programs past and present. These may be permutations of "You Are There," "This Is Your Life," "What's My Line?," "Password," etc. Some of these are obviously game shows, giving the teacher the chance to review in questions and answers the materials under study in the class. In this sense, a game of "Password" is merely a game. The players are actors only in the sense of taking part in the game, and the drama aspects are minimal. In a show-simulation such as "You are There" or "This is Your Life" the element of impromptu drama is much strongerr. During a study of Pirke Avot, it would be appropriate to organize an impromptu drama called "This is Your Life: Hillel." Students could be assigned roles as moderator, Hillel, Shammai, students of Hillel, Hillel's mom and dad, Hillel's uncle, and so on. Similarly, a game of "What's My Line?" could be organized around the various jobs held by the rabbis— shoemaker, water carrier, head of the Sanhedrin, and so on. Obviously, the better the students have mastered the material, the more learning can take place through playing out the game.

Formal Drama

Formal drama goes beyond the types which we have discussed up to this point. It requires rehearsal, and usually culminates in active presentation before an audience.

A drama may be the work of the teacher, the class, a single member of the class, or a professional. It may be an excerpt from a longer play, a one-act play, or an entire three-or-four act play. If it is to be formally presented, there are many choices of how the presentation is made. It may be memorized by the members of the group, or not. It may be presented in costume, or not. It may be presented on a formal stage, or not.

Narrated drama

In one of the simplest forms, the drama is narrated by the teacher or a single student as other students act out the parts in the story. (This narrated form is very apt for Hebrew teaching, since students must learn the vocabulary and meaning of the narration in order to properly act out their various parts.) This is a good introduction to the formal drama for all students. It provides a high degree of repetition, as the story is repeated over and over in rehearsal, and students tend to learn the story thoroughly over the course of rehearsal and presentation. Stories from the midrash and Talmud, Yiddish folk tales, Hasidic stories, and stories of incidents in the lives of American and Israeli Jews provide good material for this technique.

Shadowgraph

An alternative form to the narrated drama is the shadowgraph, in which a sheet is hung in front of the actors and a naked light bulb is mounted behind them to cast their shadows on the sheet where the shadows can be seen by the audience. The shadowgraph is a very simple form of pantomime. Usually, one narrator provides the story line, but it is possible to use the shadowgraph as a technique even as the students speak the lines.

The Formal Play

A play in which parts are taken by members of the class, rehearsed, and presented is what people normally think of as drama. Here, too, there are many choices for presentation and many opportunities for learning.

"Dramatize it, dramatize it!"—Henry James in *The Altar of the Dead.*

In its most familiar format, the play is a proscenium presentation. It is presented on a stage (usually behind the proscenium arch equipped with curtains, stage lights, and all the *accoutrements* of Broadway—on a small scale).

Alternatively, it may be presented in the theater of the classroom, in which the front of the classroom is cleared and serves as the stage. Again, the formal play may be rehearsed and then videotaped or filmed for later presentation. This has the advantage of allowing the people in the play to see themselves acting, while being free of the actual pressures of performance. Finally, the play may be a presented as a rehearsed formal reading.

Cantata

Cantatas can be handled in all the same ways as other formal plays, but the inclusion of singing requires special rehearsal and often some elaborate staging.

And while we are speaking of formal dramas, it is good to mention a few other forms. There is the mock trial, an effective way to study historical trials or debates; the pantomime, a formal play without words which attempts to convey a feeling for human emotions and actions; and the pageant, which is excellent for use in Hebrew teaching and in presenting holiday materials.

Interesting Alternatives

You may also wish to explore several other avenues of drama for the classroom.

Radio programs can be taped on a small cassette recorder and played back as presentations for other classes, parent groups, school assemblies, and the like. Using a multi-track tape recorder, sound effects and background music can be added to create a feeling of the total environment.

In similar fashion, you can take slides and/or silent films and create a sound-track for them. You can even use old filmstrips as a basis for new presentations in this way. (I don't know what else to do with all those libraries of outdated filmstrips which are extant everywhere throughout the country.)

Another alternative dramatic form is recitation. Individuals can be rehearsed for single-voiced recitation, and groups can be prepared for choral recitation. Poetry lends itself to this very nicely—and Hebrew classes can use Hebrew poetry to great advantage in recitation. Whole stories can also be divided and reworked to make effective pieces for group recitation.

There is another game which is often called "Frozen Statues" which makes for good classroom drama. In this game, students are divided into groups and asked to take poses as objects, feelings, or events. The teacher watches until the groups are somewhat ready and calls out "Freeze!" at which time everyone stops moving and tries to stand motionless while other classes or groups try to explain what is happening in the pose.

Good drama in the classroom is not restricted to the students. Teachers can dress up as characters out of history and allow themselves to be"interviewed" by the class. And teachers can extemporaneously take on a role and allow the class to discover by its questions and the teacher's responses just what the role is.

In one instance, I witnessed an entire school taking part in a mock version of the Exodus. The various classes were given places in the line of march. Older students were asked to help younger students. The principal played Moses. The teachers played the elders of the tribes. The entire school paraded around the outside grounds which had been marked off and dressed up for the occasion. At one point the confirmation class played the role of the Egyptians chasing the rest of the students across a small land bridge between two troughs of water which were flooded just after the group was across, "catching" the confirmation class in water up to their toes. The group was assembled below a small rise which became Mount Sinai. The principal went up the mountain and came back with two pieces of baked clay on which the Ten Commandments had been inscribed. In the meantime, the students had been busy building a golden calf out of paper and flour-and-water paste. The principal smashed his clay tablets and then went back up the mountain for another set. There was a fierce argument (which everyone witnessed) between the principal and a ninth grader (who was well-known for his appearances in the principal's office) and who called himself Korach. Later everyone listened as twelve confirmands reported on what they had seen in the Holy Land while they were spying. And, when all was said and done, everyone went inside to the auditorium where the tables were set for a model Seder. This was a Passover lesson that was destined to be remembered by all the students in the school. And it is a wonderful example of what drama can contribute to education.

Just as good drama in the classroom is not restricted to students, it is also not restricted to particular times of the year. Some teachers wait patiently each year for Purim to arrive before attempting to create classroom drama. By Purim time, however, it is late to admit the students to the world of dramatic activity. By Purim, the curriculum should have used drama in enough other and creative ways to make students comfortable enough to do a proper Purim *spiel*.

Chapter 11
Worship Experiences

In this chapter

Franz Rosenzweig wrote that the religious school should be an antechamber to the synagogue, preparing students for the experience of worship. He had in mind more than just those Hebrew skills which we impart to students to make them fluent in performing prayer services. The classroom is a good place to get at some of the larger concepts of prayer and ritual, even in small ways. Here, then, are eight small ways that work on any age-level.

Some years ago, I wrote a textbook called *When a Jew Prays*. It is one of many textbooks devoted to teaching the Jewish worship service, the synagogue, and the concepts of prayer Jews have given to the world at large. For Jews, prayer is no one-way street. It is more than a mere collection of words offered to God in place of ancient sacrifices. It is the poetry, history, and heritage of a literate and eloquent civilization. It includes devotions we recite to awaken ourselves to the miraculous wonders hidden in the mundane repetitions of the universe. In fact, in Jewish thought, prayer is even considered a form of study.

My teacher, the Jewish philosopher, rabbi, and educator, Eugene B. Borowitz, begins each teaching session with the tradional blessing, "Blessed are You, O Lord our God, Ruler of the Universe, Who commands us to occupy ourselves in the words of Torah." And, of course, whenever we teach as Jewish teachers, we are always involved in teaching our tradition—the Torah, in its largest sense.

We might all begin our teaching sessions in a similar manner—by saying a preliminary prayer. It would remind us all just how important are the teachings we convey to our students. Beyond that, there are other ways in which worship can be incorporated into our teaching agenda—in the Hebrew school, and in the religious school.

Worship Services

The most obvious of these is to include a brief worship service during class time. In many schools, worship services are a feature of the regular schedule. Where this is not the case, the teacher can include a service or, at the least, a prayer or two on a regular basis in the classroom. In itself, this procedure teaches the discipline of praying on a fixed schedule. To make the worship service even more of a learning experience, various students can be asked to prepare parts of the liturgy for their classmates.

In Hebrew classrooms, short worship services also serve to reinforce studies of language, language skills, and liturgy.

Conducting services

Helping students learn to lead prayer services is another reason for incorporating worship in the classroom. Using the principle of "progressive alteration," the learning can grow throughout the year as new prayers are added to those already being recited, and the worship service itself extends for slightly longer periods of time. Slowly, students will grow more and more proficient at conducting more and more of the service.

Preparing sermons

Since worship is also a form of study, the sermon is a traditional part of Jewish worship. By including it in classroom worship, teachers can help students learn to prepare brief sermons or messages which can be presented to the class as a "word of Torah," (in Hebrew, a *d'var Torah*). The presenting student learns both the skill of presentation and the content of the message being presented. Simultaneously, the class learns the content of what is presented, and develops critical listening skills.

Teachers can also ask students to base these short sermons on the units of instruction in the curriculum. In this way, sermons tie into what is being learned in the classroom, and the textbook can become the basis for preparation. This has the added advantage of allowing student sermons to become jumping-off points for text discussions.

The term "progressive alteration" is the only term I have ever coined for education. It probably stems from the fact that one or more of my Old World ancestors was a tailor. But it is easy enough to understand the principle.

When you shop for clothing for your children, you buy the clothing at least one or two sizes too large (if you are not ultra-rich, that is). Then you do a little tailoring—taking in a nip here and a tuck there. As the child grows, you do "progressive alteration," letting the clothing out bit by bit.

The best education is done in the same way. When you start the year, if you are teaching second-graders, you must keep in mind that by year's end they will be third-graders. The activities and concepts in every grade must therefore be "progressively altered" as the year goes on. If you are teaching on the same level at year's end as you did at the beginning, the students have long out grown you.

And that is what I mean by "progressive alteration."

Prayer skills

More and more, our Hebrew curriculum is concerned with the study of the basic responses and prayers of Jewish liturgy. Classroom worship can reinforce these studies by encouraging students to use the synagogue prayer book and to regularly attend services. The classroom cannot afford to be a sterile environment, separate and apart from the life of the synagogue community. Instead, it should enliven the activities of the community and be enlivened by the activities of the community. It is self-evident that prayer ranks high among the essential activities of any Jewish community. Therefore, developing prayer skills in the classroom— whether the class be a course in Hebrew or in history, ritual, or values—makes the classroom an adjunct to the synagogue's life.

Reading and discussing prayers

The prayers which we encounter in the prayer book can also become the focus of a lesson, serving as pieces in the process of set induction. For instance, the prayer for "dew and rain" can be appropriately discussed in times of drought, or in times when dew and rain are plentiful. In discussing the tallit, the prayer used when putting on the tallit can become the focus for a set-induction that initiates the lesson.

Rewriting prayers

Most prayer-oriented activities are oral; some address reading skills. A few may be writing activities. For example, students can be encouraged to rewrite in their own words (and for their own social milieu) traditional prayers which they are using. As we have seen in previous chapters, reiteration is not only a sincere form of flattery, but also a valuable exercise in learning. Prayers can be reworked as poems, or set to music, or rewritten as narratives. Depending on their age-level, students may be required to extend prayers to encompass modern themes and concerns. A prayer for peace can be rewritten to reflect our special need for peace in the post-atomic era. A prayer for freedom can encompass the modern plight of Jews in Ethiopia, in Arab lands, and in the Soviet Union. Nor is it amiss to offer up a prayer for wisdom on the day of an in-class examination.

But asking "When is God?" suggests that God is found in the moment, not in the place. Being in God's presence is not a function of where you are, but of what you are doing. The transmitter of religious sensitivity, whether parent or teacher, would then set as his task the goal of teaching children to identify those moments in their lives when God is present.
—"The Idea of God in the Jewish Classroom" by Harold Kushner in Jeffrey L. Schein and Jacob J. Staub, eds., *Creative Jewish Education*.

Writing original prayers

Every prayer service includes moments when personal devotion is in order. Jewish prayer books traditionally include personal petitions offered by the rabbis of the Talmud which can be recited when one is at a loss for some more personal prayer to offer. But there is no reason—other than lack of preparation—why one should be at a loss; and creating such prayers (even in basic Hebrew, for a Hebrew class) can become a classroom activity. There are many traditional forms which such personal prayers can take. One of the most colorful traditional forms is the acrostic, in which the opening letters of each line spell out a name or a phrase.

Creating pageantry

Last but not least, Jewish prayer is not offered in a vacuum. There are special bodily motions which make up "the dance of prayer." There are sacred objects common to all Jewish houses of worship. There are ritual movements and actions which transform the prayer service into a pageant. These can also be practiced in the classroom. And doing so adds life and meaning to their practice in the sanctuary.

What keeps prayer relevant in our lives (when it is) and motivates us to attend worship services is our understanding of both the prayers and the appurtenances of prayer. When the classroom teacher—and the teacher of adult studies—regularly includes prayer as a part of the learning process, the worship service becomes more meaningful to the study of Judaism as a whole. The time taken from other studies may be as brief as two or three minutes or as extended as twenty minutes, but it is time well spent. It tends to make a seamless whole of the study and practice of Judaism, bringing unity to classroom and synagogue.

Chapter 12
Arts & Crafts

In this chapter

There is literally no limit to what could be included in the arts and crafts chapter of a book on teaching. Arts and crafts are to the visual imagination and the right-brain modality what verbal and written skills are to the intellect and left-brain modality. Buber and Bruner (and many other educators and educational philosophers) argue that all of us are equipped with the basic skills necessary for all forms of human expression. The techniques and activities outlined in this chapter are within the scope of any classroom teacher. You can use arts and crafts in your teaching even if you have never done so before. And, if you think—for any reason—that you cannot, pretend you can; and do.

We easily accept the fact that teachers working with young children should be adept at arts and crafts. On the other hand, we equally presume that teachers working with teenagers and adults are highly qualified even if they publicly declare that they never use arts and crafts in teaching. The intimation is that the higher the age-level of the student being instructed, the less that student needs arts and crafts activities.

Nothing could be further from the truth. Most of the students we teach—from two year olds to adults—rely heavily on visual perception to form their model of the world. What they clearly see is what they most clearly understand. In fact, many things which require elaborate and arcane oral introductions are explained in simple graphic flourishes with no difficulty whatever. (Need I say that a picture is worth a thousand of these things?) When we by-pass the use of arts and crafts techniques, we only make our jobs as teachers more difficult.

Symbolic Power

The lowly classroom form which we call "arts and crafts" is much more than it seems at first glance. Whether the product of a classroom project is realistic or abstract, it is always symbolic to the person who creates it. At its very least, the created work springs from the human instinct to originate. And, depending on the maturity of the individual, it may stand for much, much more.

Arts and crafts specialists will have to look elsewhere for a more comprehensive guide to arts and crafts in the religious school. The arts and crafts activities below have been carefully and purposefully limited. Within reason, anyone should be able to complete them. Within reason, anyone should be able to incorporate them in teaching. In this book, we are concerned with activities which are enhancements to classroom learning. All of the following techniques can be applied to all ages and all subjects, including the teaching of Hebrew language.

Coloring

Coloring is often set up as an educational windmill. It is an easy target for any educator on horseback carrying a lance of wit. But, under the right conditions, coloring can be a creative experience. In media such as crayons, markers, water color, and temperas even an adult can start with an outline picture that looks like it came from a coloring book and—with a little practice—turn out a beautifully shaded piece of art.

I once observed a very skillful teacher utlizing free-form coloring. She asked students to create a translucent "stained glass window" using water colors on large sheets of heavy tracing paper. She turned on a recording of Bloch's *Jeremiah* symphony and told the students, "Listen and paint with the colors and shapes you feel the music is expressing." Thus, she allowed them to use two perceptual senses; gave them a taste of a rare form of Jewish music; and created a memorable Jewish experience—all at the same time.

Another way to turn coloring into something greater than itself is to prepare an outline picture of a key scene from some story or circumstance being studied. Ask students to color in the outline as the story is being told or read aloud. For those who take part in this activity, the process is a little like creating a color animation, since the event literally "takes on color" as the story proceeds.

Creativity, as has been said, consists largely of rearranging what we know in order to find out what we do not know. ... Hence, to think creatively we must be able to look afresh at what we normally take for granted.
—Kneller, George, *The Art and Science of Creativity* (New York: Holt, Rinehart and Winston, 1965).

Drawing

Coloring is filling in prepared outlines. Drawing, on the other hand, involves preparing the art itself. It requires a degree of technical skill at its higher levels. But, as a classroom activity, the level of achievement is usually not an issue. Since drawing is always and only done on the artist's level, there is no impediment to its use with any age student.

Media available for drawing range from pencil to charcoal to paints to chalk to pastels, and everything in between. Students can be encouraged to draw realistically or in the abstract.

Whatever the curriculum for the course, drawing can be a useful adjunct. It can be used as an element in set induction, as a review of materials covered, or as a means to personalize data. Students can draw representations of historical events, illustrations for stories or poetry, covers for class reports, etc. One thing you can count on in drawing is that the work is never mindless. It requires a degree of concentration and thought which helps to solidify the learning of any classroom material.

Classroom murals

Drawing things together as a class is the next step after drawing itself. A long sheet of butcher paper spread out on a table or on the floor can become the focal point for a motivational activity or a review as it turns into a classroom mural. The mural can then be hung in the classroom where it continues to be a reminder of the unit of instruction in which it was produced.

Copying

If it can be drawn, it can be copied. And there is an infinite number of activities which can be designed around copying. Many textbooks in use today are filled with beautiful illustrations and photographs, often in fullcolor. Some Jewish magazines include illustration. And album-type books on Jewish life, art, and civilization abound. It is an embarrassment of riches.

Even so, finding just the right image for a particular moment in a particular lesson is not always possible. We may locate the costume of the Maccabees in a book on Jewish costumes through the ages, find the site of Modi'in in a tour guide to Israel, discover the shape and detailing of the short sword in a book on ancient weaponry, and so on. Then we can rely on the students' imaginations to bring these bits and pieces of visual information together, or we

Several major scientists have reported that they conceived their solutions to problems through visualization of the problems. Morton Hunt, in his book *The Universe Within* tells how Einstein reconciled his theory of relativity with Newtonian physics in just this way. He "pictured a box falling freely down a very long shaft; inside it, an occupant took coins and keys out of his pocket and let them go. The objects, Einstein saw, remained in midair, alongside him, because they were falling at the same rate as he—a situation temporarily identical with being in space, beyond any gravitational field. From this visual construct, Einstein was able to sense some of those seemingly contradictory relationships about movement and rest, acceleration and gravity, that he later put into mathematical and verbal form in his general theory of relativity."

can bring the material to life by asking students to copy the elements, thereby creating a picture of the whole.

By copying the outlines of portraits from photographs, we can create representations of people being studied which can become the foundation of a bulletin board display for the current unit. And the copying of illustrations from textbooks can be used similarly.

Copying and tracing share many of the same attributes, with tracing sometimes being the more satisfying of the two approaches. For classroom activities, it is best to buy a slightly heavier tracing paper than the local dime store stocks. School suppliers and art stores generally carry the heavier tracing stock. It does not tear so frequently; and because you do not have to be afraid of tearing you can produce a sharper image.

Tracing maps and locating new details on them is a sure way of making historical geography more exciting. For example, a map of Europe and North Africa can lead to an interesting lesson in the distribution of Jews throughout the Roman Empire following the Bar Kokhba wars.

Small groups can copy parts of maps in giant sizes for classroom display and use. These can be illustrated with figures traced or copied from other sources, and updated as units of instruction progress.

It is also good to keep in mind that many students who feel shy about their talents at drawing feel right at home when copying or tracing.

Creating calendars and time-lines

One of the most meaningful and useful arts and crafts activities is the creation of calendars and time-line charts. People process time in two different ways as they mature. Before their teenage years, most children cannot conceive of chronology in absolute terms. They may hear a date such as 1948 or 70 C.E. or 576 B.C.E. and get nothing more than a sense of long ago and far away. For young children, all dates prior to their birth date generally are "**B.G.**"—"Before Grandparents." This does not mean that young children are unequipped to deal with history. Young or old, we all have a built-in means of coping with time, and that is *sequence*. Even the youngest child can learn who comes first and who comes next. Therefore dates of the reigns of Saul, David, and Solomon may have little meaning to a young child, but the sequence—(1) Saul, (2) David, and (3) Solomon—is easily learned by normal students at any age.

As we mature, we begin to translate sequence into

As we mature, we begin to translate sequence into *chronology*. This is no easy process, except for those with a mathematical bent, and it may continue well into adulthood. In fact, some people never fully make the transition. For the purposes of Jewish history, which we teach in religious school for the concepts and values it represents, the transition makes no difference at all. Sequence and chronology are both acceptable means to understanding when things happened.

Here is the classic case, however, of the advantage of pictures over words. Dates, and words describing sequence, are much less effective than a simple daily schedule, calendar, or time-line. (It would be extraordinarily strange to try to deal with an appointment book or monthly calendar laid out in words as opposed to grids. Even the most avid reader would not want to plough through a long series of sentence stems like "At five o'clock p.m. on the first day of March, I will_____ .")

Although there are a few commercial illustrated time-lines available to the Jewish school, none of them will be as effective as a time-line created by the students for the unit of study in which they are involved. In the same way, a prominently displayed calendar of that unit of study can help both teachers and students to focus on completing the materials within a structured amount of time.

Time-lines and calendars can partake of all the media and activities above. They can be made to extend across an entire wall of the classroom, designed to run along the ceiling of the classroom from front to back or side to side, or constructed as single sides of standard typing paper to be hole-punched and kept in a notebook.

Students working in small groups can be encouraged to chart the schedule for the work they are to accomplish, to make a time-line as a part of their reports, or to establish a visual sequence of events in a story or historical incident.

Since this is a common area for the use of arts and crafts, a couple of examples should suffice. In studying the waves of immigration in which modern European Jews returned to Israel, students could be asked to create a time-line indicating the names of each "Aliyah" and the countries from which the Jews came. However, in studying the Six-Day War, a time-line would be even less instructive than a daily calendar. And, to combine activity with activity, the daily calendar could consist of maps of the State of Israel with changes in the status of armies and borders shown for each day of the war.

Time-lines and calendars are wonderful instruments for teaching. They are truly among the few activities in which students of any age can engage in the original process of creation, and, in later sessions, enjoy, embellish, and benefit from the fruits of their labors.

Greeting cards

Our students live in a highly visual society. We have already noted some of the intensity of the visual in seeing that television helps to create the modern myths by which we live. What is vivid is what can be seen, pictured, imaged, and verified through the visual sense. The Jewish classroom cannot, at any time, afford to be aloof or apart from this modern truth. The tendency of teachers of Judaism to be literal and highly verbal rather than visual in their approach only diminishes the importance of what they are teaching in the eyes of their students for whom visualization is a primary learning tool (witness MTV, for example). We do not normally require students to adjust their maturity to meet the maturity of the teacher, nor to adjust their priorities to match the priorities of their teachers. Only in this instance—verbalization versus visualization—do we insist that our way is the only proper way. But, as we do this, we lose rapport with the students. And losing rapport is the last thing we want. Do you *see* what I am driving at?

Another arts and crafts activity which produces a great deal of enjoyment is the creation of appropriate greeting cards. The standard holy days provide a number of good times for the creation of cards. You may also consider asking the class to make cards and visit when one member of the group has an extended illness, has a new baby brother or sister, is moving to another city, has a Bar or Bat Mitzvah, or celebrates some special family occasion. I even knew one teacher who had the class make cards to wrap around their report cards, and another teacher who culminated a study of Soviet Jewry with greeting cards to Refuseniks trapped in the Soviet Union. All of these cards teach useful lessons in Jewish values and social consciousness.

You can also use greeting cards as an imaginative teaching device. What kind of card and what kind of message would Ben Gurion send to Jerusalemites during the siege of Jerusalem? What kind of card and what kind of message would Rashi have sent to the victims of the Crusades? What kind of card and what kind of message would the the six days of the week send to the Sabbath?

Decorating the classroom

Above we spoke of classroom murals and other arts and crafts activities which could be incorporated into classroom decor. That is just the beginning. Bare walls and windows should be viewed as a challenge to your teaching creativity. If you like, you can use commercially prepared decorations for holidays or units of instruction. If you do this, you can still ask students to help in the actual decorating process.

Alternatively, the decoration of the classroom can become an organic part of your teaching process. You can plan arts and crafts activities which illuminate your teaching and aid students in the process of discovery learning. These can be put on display while the unit is being taught (or until the holiday is over) and then removed and sent home with the students. If the display becomes elaborate enough, it can be transferred as an exhibit to a larger space (an auditorium or group meeting room) and shared with other classes or parents.

And, while you are considering bare walls and windows, remember the ceiling, too. Mobiles hung from above can be one of the most effective elements of a classroom display.

Maps, charts and diagrams

We have already mentioned maps several times. But they are so important to learning that they deserve a special discussion. Historically, Jews were among the great mapmakers of Portugal employed by Prince Henry—the mapmakers who made possible the navigation and charting of the world's oceans. We need not expect that this talent will extend to the students in our classrooms. But we can be fairly certain that almost everyone has some interest in maps and the making of maps. During the nearly two thousand years of the Diaspora, Jews have visited and lived in nearly every nook and cranny of the world. And this adds another dimension to natural interest.

Maps can be used for purposes of simple location, for showing population shifts, for demonstrating distances, for showing geologic features which have influenced human behavior, and for a myriad of other purposes. Commercially available maps include tracings of events such as Abraham's wanderings, the Exodus, the Crusades, the Holocaust, and more. These can be studied as is (remember to have on hand a protractor and a ruler). Sometimes an outline map may be available on which to base a project or activity. But student-drawn maps are the real optimum. Even though these may be out-of-scale, they provide a degree of flexibility which no commercial map can match.

As with maps, charts and graphs drawn by the students can make points which would take forever to bring home by verbal means. A good example is a bar graph of the major waves of immigration of Jews to the United States. The first (Sephardic) immigration figures will produce a very short bar. The second and third (western European) migration figures will be represented by significantly longer bars. The fourth (eastern European) migration will produce a bar that literally shoots off the edge of the paper by comparison.

Making costumes, scenery, and backdrops

When you are working with formal drama, the opportunity also exists for using arts and crafts to plan and make costumes, scenery, and backdrops. You can divide the class into groups to create the various elements needed for the drama, or everyone can work together on a master plan.

Rudolph Arnheim once experimented by asking his students to do "think-by" drawings. He gave them terms and concepts such as "Past, Present, and Future," "Democracy," and "Good and Evil" and asked them to draw these subjects. He called these drawings "non-mimetic"—bearing no likeness to objects or events.

You might try this with your students to see how they would draw such subjects as "Freedom," "Torah" (but not the physical scroll), "Prayer" (but not the physical act of praying), and "Image of God" (but not a physical image).

The resulting drawings can be verbalized and analyzed—they can be treated as symbolic representations. They might even make for a different and creative exhibition—one which goes beyond the normal realm of student art.

As you study new units, consider the possibilities of costume as a means of helping students visualize and typify an era or a culture. There are wonderful resources available in this area, from books devoted to Jewish costuming to artistic renderings of costumes in textbooks and storybooks.

Some teachers of young children also keep a dress-up box in the classroom, adding costumes to it from time to time. During freeplay students can be encouraged to try on costumes from the dress-up box and have fun reviewing stories and lessons.

Shoe-box dioramas

Another way of depicting events or scenes is through miniaturization. A simple shoe box with a frame cut out of one end or side can become a three-dimensional diorama. Scissors and construction paper, some tagboard, odd pieces of fabric, twigs and fallen leaves, and the like are all the materials one needs to create these primitive imitations of the art of Faberge. Primitive or not, there is something about looking at little things in perspective that makes the final product pleasing. And the act of creating a miniature world can teach a great deal about nearly any subject from Passover to the shtetl.

Creating books and book covers

One of the nearly lost arts of publishing is the art of creating a fine "blurb" for a book—a brief summary of the contents, a summary which entices one to read the book. In creating the jacket design for books as an art project, you could also ask students to exercise their writing skills in cooking up eloquent "blurbs" for the flyleaves of the book's jacket.

In some congregations, students approaching Bar and Bat Mitzvah are encouraged to copy out their Torah portions by hand and to illuminate their copies. This is in imitation of the Jewish tradition that each person should make a complete copy of the entire Torah text. In today's world, few Jews take the time to complete this massive task. But the idea is a wonderful one, nonetheless. And we can replicate it in other, lesser ways.

Students can be encouraged to keep illustrated diaries, sketch-books, collections of pictures cut from periodicals, photograph albums, etc. These can be illuminated and hand-bound with report covers, brads, or staples. The covers can be decorated, too.

Small group and committee reports can be assigned to be completed in the same way and put on display at the end of a unit of instruction.

Remember to encourage students to imitate the opening pages of books, by placing their names prominently as authors, and showing photo credits and other credits on the back of the title page. I can testify to the pleasure which authorship brings, and I highly recommend it to everyone. Of the making of books, there should be no end.

Photos

Nearly every student has a camera and many subjects in the religious school lend themselves nicely to photography. Holidays are wonderful subjects for a roll of film, as are the interior of the sanctuary and the exteriors of local synagogues and Jewish institutions. Students can use the photographs to prepare photo-essays, to illustrate verbal reports, as illustrations in written reports, or to mount an exhibit for other classes or for other adults. Transparencies can be made into a slide show and combined with background music and narration.

In Hebrew language classes, writing Hebrew words on the backs of photos can make a very effective set of personal flashcards for learning the meaning of words in a way that goes beyond mere translation.

Teachers can also take photos of students doing arts and crafts activities to display alongside the student creations, adding an extra dimension to the work and exhibition of arts and crafts. And, if the group becomes a close-knit unit over the course of the year, a class photo can be a nice memento.

Designing certificates and awards

Students can design their own certificates and awards. These need not replace commercially available certificates, which are well-designed and motivationally sound. But student-designed certificates can enhance units of instruction directly. "Imagine and create a certificate that might be presented to the Baal Shem Tov for his years of service to the community," might be one such assignment. Or, "Design and create an award to be given to Deborah the Judge for her bravery in battle." Or, "Design and letter a Hebrew certificate for the celebration of Israel's Independence Day." Or, "Design and make an award to be given to everyone who searches for the afikomen at the end of this year's Passover Seder."

You will want to keep your sense of humor very much alive during this process. Humorous certificates and awards can teach as much as serious ones, and can be a lot more fun to create. How about a certificate to honor Honi the Circle-Maker for stubbornness? Or an award to Abraham for striking the best bargain with God on the issue of the destruction of cities?

Study Jewish art and artists

Last, but not least, arts and crafts can be extended outward to the incorporation of the study of Jewish art and artisans. The synagogue gift shop is a resource full of contemporary examples of Jewish art in the form of *mezuzot, tallitot, tefillin,* boxes for *etrog,* candle holders for *Shabbat, kiddush* cups, *menorot,* Passover plates, and a host of other examples. In studying history, Jewish art and architecture can play an important role. In studying, ritual and customs, Jewish *objets d'art* can be explored and examined. From ancient to modern times, Jewish symbols have occupied a central role in Jewish life and manners.

Media and Symbols

The Elements of Style

Designer Joe Molloy views *designing* and *writing* as parallel strategies. ...Molloy recommends applying the ideas expressed in the famous little book by Theodore Strunk and E. B. White, **The Elements of Style**...

Some of Strunk and White's rules for writers that Molloy applies to design are the following:

Omit needless words.
Place yourself in the background.
Revise and rewrite.
Do not overwrite.
Do not overstate.
Do not affect a breezy manner.
Be clear.
Write in a way that comes naturally.
Work from a suitable design.
Make sure the reader knows who is speaking.
—Edwards, Betty, *Drawing on the Artist Within* (New York: Simon & Schuster, Inc., 1986).

Media and symbols are primary words in the teaching vocabulary of the master teacher. The strength of media and symbol in combination is legend. Many Jews are involuntarily shocked when they first encounter a traditional Navajo rug. a primary Navajo motif is the repetition of a twisted cross—and it is only natural for Jews to react with some degree of revulsion to a figure they know as the swastika, the symbol of Nazi Germany. In this regard, at least, Jews and Navajos are clearly not members of the same tribe.

In one of my master teacher workshops, I begin a segment by drawing an equilateral triangle on the chalkboard. The medium is chalk. The symbol is a triangle.

I ask teachers to imagine how this triangle can be used to represent Judaism. The answers vary.

Almost always, people offer the classic Jewish triad: "God," "Torah," and "Israel." This triad derives from a quotation in the Zohar but it has become a standard organizational divice for studying Judaism.

Pressed a little harder, people recall the famous quotation of Hillel from *The Sayings of the Elders*: "If I am not for myself, who will be for me? If I am only for myself, what am I? And, if not now, when?" It so happens that I once wrote an entire book on Jewish ethics (*When a Jew Seeks Wisdom*) using this particular triad as the unit divisions. Pressed even further, someone quotes Simon ben Gamaliel's triad, from the same classic text, "The world depends on three things: On Torah, on Service to God, and on works of lovingkindness." I could easily have written the same book on ethics using these three categories as basic divisions.

If they have studied with me for any length of time, the people in the workshop are probably also familiar with another triadic representation of Jewish life—Franz Rosenzweig's conceptualization of the basic Jewish themes as "Creation," "Revelation," and "Redemption."

Some will be familiar with the corollary part of Rozensweig's thesis in his classic work of Jewish philosophy, *The Star of Redemption*. Rosenzweig points to three "pagan" points which also form an equilateral triangle, and which are also essentials in Jewish life, namely, "God," "the universe," and "humanity." When the two equilateral triangles are superimposed—one turned upside-down on the other—they form the "star" of redemption—a six-pointed "Star of David."

Other people use the triangle on the chalkboard to visualize the relationships in the classroom—"teacher," "pupil," and "curriculum." Still others point to the three patriarchs, "Abraham," "Isaac," and "Jacob." And son on.

When the group has completed the exercise by naming as many of Judaism's triads as they can, I move to another part of the chalkboard and draw a square. Now we begin to delineate all the quadrangular relationships which Judaism has created through the ages from the four types of individuals outlined in *The Sayings of the Elders* to the four species used on Sukkot and how each represents a character type, to the four cups of wine on Passover and the promises each cup is said to represent.

By this time, the point is driven home. It is not the specific triangle or square that you draw on the chalkboard that makes this deep impression. It is, instead, the symbolic and graphic use of a spare or a triangle (or a chart or a map or any graphic, by extension) which is important. It is only natural that people should refer to geometric shapes and graphic images as mnemonics—aids to the memory. In fact, the very ideological power of there being ten central commandments may lie in the fact that we can count to ten on the fingers of our two hands! What simpler device for memory could there be?

All this adds up to one final message regarding the use of arts and crafts in teaching: It is not just a skill that students should develop. The teacher who uses graphic symbols and representations can enhance the learning curve of the class significantly, makes studies more vivid and real, and enable the vast majority of the group to visualize the meaning of a lesson or unit accurately.

Chapter 13
Music

In this chapter

Students today may be strangers to spelling, have a mere passing acquaintance with grammar, be nearly inadequate at arts and crafts, and be barely on speaking terms with their mother tongue. But they know music. Below you will find musical activities that even the nonmusical teacher can use; and a note about extracurricular time and what it can mean to a teacher.

Every people has its music. We do not want to make exaggerated claims for the Jewish people. Nevertheless, Jewish music just happens to include the music of nearly every other people. Through the centuries, Jews picked up musical styles everywhere they lived and made them their own.

You can use Jewish music in your classroom and never run out of materials. And, of course, music soothes the savage breast—which, in the case of many adolescent classrooms, may mean most of the students being taught. If you need further proof of this point, just note that it is adolescents, more than any other group, who make or break musical fashions.

DO I HAVE TO BE MUSICAL?

Most teachers worry about the fact that they are not musical. As with arts and crafts, they tend to leave music to a specialist, if a specialist is available, or to do without it entirely. But through the years I have found that even nonmusical teachers can use a few of these techniques effectively.

Singing as a group

Initially, the most difficult technique is leading students in group singing. Group participation in song is best when singing is led with a guitar, an accordion, or a piano. This means that either the teacher or someone in the class must be willing to learn songs in advance, and to lead and accompany them.

> Song is the soul of the universe. The throne of God breathes music; even the four letters, *Yod, He, Vav, He,* that spell the name of God are four musical notes.
> —Rabbi Naḥman of Bratzlav

You can also use records and prerecorded cassette tapes to lead group singing. These require less talent, but a willingness on the part of the teacher to sing along. Their use also requires some planning. You have to know exactly where on the record the song you wish to sing is located; and, with tapes, it is always best to transfer to a single tape the songs you wish to use in the exact order in which you wish to use them.

Group singing as a classroom technique additionally requires you to tie the music directly to the curriculum of study. This is obviously easy to do with certain simple Hebrew songs, with holiday melodies, and with Israeli songs (when teaching about Israel). It is more difficult to plan for songs which relate to topics in history, values, and other conceptual studies, but even here it can be done if you persist.

There is one more thing to remember. The first time is the hardest time. Music and dance both require the teacher to "break the ice." Groups which do not regularly sing together, have a hard time beginning the process. But after one or two times singing together every group will find it natural. As with getting students to read, the most important thing is consistency on the part of the teacher. If the teacher continues to require it to happen, it will eventually become a natural part of what happens in the classroom.

Listening to Jewish music

My mind seems to have become a kind of machine for grinding general laws out of large collections of facts... If I had to live my life again, I would make a rule to read some poetry and listen to some music at least once each week; for perhaps the parts of my brain now atrophied would thus have been kept active through use.
—Charles Darwin, cited in H. Read, *Education through Art.*

Singing together is just one way in which Jewish music can enter the classrooom. After all, there is a wide range of Jewish music out there, from Jewish theater music to Israeli music, from cantorial music to folk music. Listening to selections can help students to gain a deeper appreciation not just for the music of their people, but also for particular points in the curriculum.

If you are studying Shabbat, for example, you can ask students to listen to a cantorial version of the *Kiddush* and compare it with a recording of Kurt Weill's theatrical *Kiddush*. If you are studying American Jewish history, you could ask students to listen to music by American Jewish composers such as Irving Berlin and Leonard Bernstein. Studying eastern European Jewry might be the occasion for hearing Yiddish folk music; and studying Oriental Jewry would make an occasion for listening to a recording of a Yemenite Seder. All these are readily available. And a cassette recorder is the only tool you will need to use them in the classroom.

Five to ten minutes of listening (depending on attention spans) is all that most classes can bear. But this may be extended as the group expands its listening skills.

Always set the stage for the music before turning it on. Let the students know what they are about to listen to, what they should be listening for, or how they should listen (quietly, eyes closed, while they do something else, etc.). Afterwards, you can choose to discuss the music or not. If you decide to discuss it, you can lead the discussion to the style of the music, to a comparison of several different styles, to how the music relates to the subject matter, to the choice of music, or to any of a dozen other possibilities.

Studying Jewish musicians

Another occasion for listening is when studying a famous Jewish musician or composer. Composers such as Bloch and Mahler, or musicians like Stern and Rubenstein have been recorded extensively. Some of their works fit particularly well with various religious school studies. For example, consider Bernstein's *Jeremiah* symphony, which can be used in conjunction with the teaching of the prophets. Other works can be studied just because they are a part of the tradition of Jewish music and musicianship. Again, you will want to follow the rules for listening outlined above—setting the stage, presenting the music, and discussing or processing it afterward. In conjunction with arts and crafts, I mentioned an exercise which works very well during the listening phase. That is to allow students to draw or color at the time the music is playing, using the feelings and emotions which the music elicits as the basis for what is drawn or the colors being used. Similarly, you can ask students to write poetry or jot down random thoughts as the music plays. This technique makes the listening a little more activity-centered, and allows students to exercise their own creativity.

Creating song parodies

Even teachers with no musical training can ask students to create song parodies as a class activity. By replacing the words to well-known songs—like *"Oh, Susanna,"* *"Yesterday," "On Top of Old Smokey,"* and others—students can create Jewish versions that deal with almost any Jewish subject that is being taught. Some classic parodies have gained a sort of life of their own—for example, the *"Ballad of the Four Sons"* sung to the tune of *"O My Darling, Clementine,"* and the "Jewish" version of *"Puff, the Magic Dragon,"* called *"Puff, the Kosher Dragon."*

Listen to Whom?

Just as a "for-example," here's a list of ten major Jewish violinists whose recordings have been recently available:

Jascha Heifetz
Leonid B. Kogan
Yehudi Menuhin
Nathan Milstein
David Oistrakh
Itzhak Perlman
Alexander Schneider
Isaac Stern
Joseph Szigeti
Pinchas Zuckerman

Music and sound effects also provide a direct means of teaching basic skills. For example, *Sesame Street*'s curriculum includes "auditory discrimination," one subcategory being "sound identification: the child can associate sounds with familiar objects or animals, *ex.*, car, horn, wood, saw, moo of a cow." Here sound effects can provide a direct teaching device.
—Gerald S. Lesser, *Children and Television: Lessons from Sesame Street.* (New York: Random House, 1974).

In fact, Lesser points out nearly 46 background music modalities which children recognize before they are even in school—such as "magical-occurrence music," "racing music," "escape music," "near-miss music," "gathering-storm music," "start-of-a-long journey music," and so on.

What kinds of Jewish musical "cues" do your students immediately recognize?

Now listen to the opening bars of the second movement of Leonard Bernstein's *Symphony No. 1 (Jeremiah)*... Does it sound familiar? Its key is different... but essentially it is a straightforward statement of the traditional Ashkenazic cantillation of *Nevi-im*(Prophets). Listen to Bernstein's entire second movement. Fragments of the chant appear again and again, twisted and stretched out, its odd rhythms creating the effect of restlessness and turmoil which the composer had in mind.

The same accents, applied to the same words in the same passage of Jeremiah... have an entirely different musical interpretation in the Sephardic cantillation. —Judith Eisenstein, *Heritage of Music: The Music of the Jewish People* (New York: UAHC, 1972).

Likewise, students can use well-known television and radio advertising jingles to "advertise" a Jewish concept or holiday.

This is also an excellent activity for Hebrew classes. Students can extend their vocabularies by using the words in song parodies and choosing"helping" words from student dictionaries.

Creating "psalms"

In a more serious vein, Jewish liturgical music can be used as the basis for composing English-language lyrics that convey the underlying message of the original prayers. These new English-language versions can then be made a part of the classroom prayer service and serve a double teaching purpose. You can also ask the class to begin with a modern melody or folk melody and compose a Hebrew or English prayer lyric.

Studying traditional modes

Most traditional Jewish music is available on record or tape. In fact, in a *tour de force*, Saul Wachs, a leading Jewish educator from Philadelphia, has even recorded the traditional liturgical chant for the entire prayer service. There are many recordings of shorter selections, too, including the Four Questions for the Pesah Seder, music for blessings, the music of the major congregational responses in worship, etc.

As the occasion arises in the classroom, these can be played and taught. The teacher who is musically inclined can forego the recorded versions and teach these melodies directly. Such lessons are always appropriate in the Hebrew school, but they also work well in many other subjects traditionally taught in the religious school.

As with all the above, the closer the connection you draw between what you are teaching in general and the music in particular, the more meaningful the musical activity.

Dancing

Teaching Jewish dance has nearly always been the realm of the specialist. Subjects such as Hebrew and Israel lend themselves naturally to short dance periods. In cases where specialists aren't available, teachers can fill in very successfully. Most teachers can learn a dance without too much difficulty.

One good reason for going to all this bother is that religious school students very often are involved in private dance classes. (Older students are often good dancers. Some are trained in Israeli or Jewish dance. And some may be willing to lead short dance sessions for you.)

Dancing is also an excellent way of allowing students to let off steam when the class begins to act out. If you are a talented dancer, you can use dance as a form of classroom management. And, if you can tie it in to the materials you are studying, you can derive a double benefit.

All of this aside, it is also very important that we guard our heritage of dance alongside our heritage of song. The classroom can be an important part of this process.

Finding resources on Jewish dance—published books, especially—is no easy matter. You will come across two or three of these, if you look hard enough. And each of them is worth its weight in gold. For the record (no pun intended), the finest of them all was a pioneering effort done before Israel was even a state! It was called *Palestine Dances*. If your synagogue is old enough, there may be a precious copy lurking in the library.

Performing song and dance

If the subject matter of a course allows for song and dance, then it also allows for performance. Rehearsed song and dance—even the amateur choir and dance troupe—can be a refreshing change from the usual verbal presentations at assemblies, open school days, and other occasions. Most teachers will not take time during class to prepare for performances. But students often willingly volunteer to prepare outside class time.

An Aside

This brings me to a point which I have skirted many times in this volume. Teaching—master teaching, that is—is not a paid profession. No one can pay you enough to make you want to be a master teacher.

Most teachers spend an average of one hour of preparation for each hour of class time. The master teachers I have known make it a practice to spend far longer. I regularly set aside three hours of preparation for each hour of class time that I will be teaching—even when I am teaching a lesson which I could basically do by rote.

Do not misunderstand. I do not spend three hours of preparation in a slavish fashion. I begin by checking over or creating my outline. I usually find something that could be improved. This leads me to my resource shelf, or to the library, or to one of many telephone resources. In my search, my eyes light upon something else that is interesting. The investigation intensifies. I find myself engrossed. I look at my watch. Two and a half-hours have passed. Did I finish preparing my class? Not quite. I return to the basics. But *the places I have been in the meantime!* It makes preparation downright enjoyable.

An aside to this aside

You may think I have forgotten that this is a chapter on music in the classroom. Not so.

I will now return to the subject—in general and in specific.

Performing song and dance (continued ...)

Preparing a choir or a dance troupe may mean putting in hours outside the classroom. The idea of all that extra time seems burdensome, but like the preparation time I set aside, it will reward you manyfold. Minutes and hours spent with your students outside of class are nearly always ones you will remember fondly. Teaching in this extracurricular atmosphere will give your students a chance to be personal. Your students will teach you—about themselves, about their world, about the future of our world together. As it turns out, students all too soon become colleagues. They go out and do important things. But they, like you, will remember those choir and dance rehearsals. They will treasure moments spent with you outside of class, and the special attention you gave them.

And, whether you meet outside of class for choir and dance rehearsals, or drama groups, or bulletin board decorating projects, or committee meetings, or any of a thousand extracurricular activities—even for your own learning during extended preparation times—these are moments that count in a special way.

Chapter 14
Field Trips and Collecting

In this chapter

Collecting and field trips may at first seem strange partners. But not when you examine them closely. Collecting is a way of bringing the world outside the classroom inside the classroom. Field trips take the classroom outside to the world. Both work in unique ways to make your classroom walls semipermeable.

In teaching you can take every inclination, talent, and impulse you have and somehow adapt it to the classroom. But some impulses normally lie beyond the classroom walls. You must either bring them into the classroom or get the class out there to witness them.

Collecting miniaturizes a subject, scaling it down so that it can easily be studied. Field tripping plunks you down in the midst of a subject, allowing you to experience it. Collecting is controlled. It can easily be manipulated to meet your teaching necessities. Field tripping is normally beyond your personal control. You can only estimate its anticipated benefits. Of course, in the final analysis, both depend largely on how you, as the teacher, utilize them. And, as with all teaching, you can "retrofit" a bad experience with a meaningful discussion to create a good lesson.

When a field trip is scheduled outside the school or synagogue, there are some basic guidelines that must be followed. First, remember to send home a permission slip for parents to sign. The exact form of this permission slip is usually worked out and standardized by the school. Second, all the details must be arranged in advance with the place to be visited. These details include the date, the time of arrival and departure, the number of children and/or adults in your group, what you want to see, and whether you require a guide or interpreter. Third, make sure that appropriate transportation is arranged. Fourth, collect any money that may be involved in the field trip. Last, keep a list of students

When I say that you cannot control the experience of a field trip, I am being what a Nashville Federation lady called *tahlitic* (an Americanization for the Yiddishism meaning "down to earth"): A fourth grade teacher I know took her students to the Museum of Natural History. On the bus, coming back to the school, she overheard one nine-year-old say to his friend, "Do you know why we went to see that dead circus?"

and whether or not their fees and permission slips are in. You will want to telephone the home of any student who has not completed the necessary arrangements to insure maximum participation.

Some teachers wait for the school or the principal to suggest a field trip. I suggest a more aggressive approach. Seek out an opportunity for least one field trip with your class each year. Even in "lean years," when it seems nothing of consequence is taking place in the community, you can usually make something happen. Here are a few good examples:

Visiting the synagogue sanctuary

Creating a geography of Jewish life could begin in the sanctuary. It is rife with symbols that remind us of the Temple, of religious observance, of cultic customs, and the like. You may wish to ask students to draw a map of a sanctuary, including a legend that gives some brief background on each of the many things that are needed to complete the map.

Getting out of the classroom as far as the synagogue sanctuary is a simple thing. Yet every sanctuary is full of potential experiences, and makes a perfect field trip for preschoolers, young elementary students, and occasionally even adolescents and adults. A tour with the rabbi, cantor, or synagogue historian (this may be any adult synagogue member, preferably one who knows the history of the synagogue) can make a memorable and lasting impression. It can also enhance those times when students attend worship services by giving students a basic familiarity with the sanctuary and its symbols.

This activity is appropriate for students studying Hebrew, prayer, synagogue, symbols, and holidays, in other words, virtually all students in the religious school and many students in adult courses.

If the synagogue includes a *beit midrash* where adults regularly gather to study Talmud and other rabbinic sources, or a ritual bath or *mikveh*, you may wish to visit these facilities as well.

Visiting the synagogue cemetery

Adults and adolescents can also visit the synagogue cemetery. In many places, the cemetery (often, the "old" cemetery) is now an historical wonder.

My family will always remember the time we visited the cemetery of the Charleston synagogue—one of the oldest synagogues in the Western Hemisphere. We had the good fortune to be led through this visit by a former president of the synagogue who knew the history of the Jewish community in Charleston and knew what were the most interesting points to be seen in the cemetery. We read flowery poetry from eighteenth-century headstones, found the graves of those who died in the Revolution and those who died in the Civil War (and noted how young they were when they died), compared the many graves of children below the age of two to the relatively small number of such graves today, and generally heard the entire history of Charleston (and, I might add, American Jewry) from the grave markers of those who lived it.

While visiting the average synagogue cemetery may not provide a comparably rich experience, nearly every synagogue cemetery tells a unique Jewish story. Typically, Jewish cemeteries include the graves of those whose names have become household words in the community—those who established the large department stores, who donated to the building of parts of the synagogue, who developed tracts of land that still bear their names in the streets or avenues, and so on. Poetry on gravestones is found in nearly all cemeteries, and other inscriptions give insight to the personal lives and sometimes tragic deaths of those they commemorate.

On a visit to the synagogue cemetery you can teach students the Jewish custom of placing a pebble on the top of a headstone to mark your visit to it. And you can conclude a cemetery field trip by reciting the *Kaddish* prayer together as a group, a particularly moving moment.

Be forewarned, however, that there are some sensitive issues involved in visiting a cemetery. Some parents—and, occasionally, some students—object to cemetery visits. Some may be prohibited from such visits by virtue of being observant *kohanim*, members of the Jewish priestly class. Special provisions should be made for these class members, and alternatives offered to them. And proper decorum must, of course, be maintained at all times. Graves should be respected and honored.

But, all in all, a visit to a synagogue burial ground can be a positive and meaningful learning experience for students studying life cycle, prayer, Hebrew (especially Hebrew names), and Jewish customs and ceremonies.

Visiting other synagogues

An apocryphal story tells of two Jews who were shipwrecked and stranded on a deserted island. Some years later a passing boat saw their signal and came to rescue them. Before leaving the island, the Jews offered to show the ship's captain around. The captain was amazed to see that they had built three synagogues. When he inquired, the first Jew pointed to one synagogue and said, "That's where I worship." The second Jew pointed to the second building

How We Explore

Jerome Bruner has distinguished three effective means we use in exploring situations:

1. By performances: fingerings, trials, searchings, etc. These are termed *enactions*.
2. Through imagery: icons, illustrations, etc. These are termed *depictions*.
3. Through oral expressions and verbalizations. These are termed *sentences*.

In doing field trips, the teacher should particularly seek out places and things which allow for the ultimate use of all three of these means.

and said, "That's where I worship." Then they both pointed at the third synagogue and, in unison, said, "We would't dream of setting foot in that synagogue."

Most towns with two or more Jews have more than one synagogue. Visiting a synagogue other than your own for comparison can be a stimulating field trip. Some synagogues have balconies that were originally used for (or still may be used for) women; some have a *mehitza* to separate men and women; some are built in the Sephardic style; some feature ornate architecture; some contain elaborate organs; and there may be a host of other unique and identifying features. Every one of these features can tell volumes about Judaism. To the credit of American Jewry, nearly all synagogues have at least one other feature which is unique—namely, the rabbi. Always ask if the rabbi is willing and available to lead your group's tour.

Visiting local churches

Everything that has been said about visiting synagogues is true of visiting churches. Hearing what other people believe has a way of reaffirming one's own beliefs. Of course, all religions have value—otherwise they could hardly attract adherents. But when you cross the fence and take a close look at the grass on the other side, it nearly always appears less green than you expected.

A visit to a Catholic church, for example, and a guided walk around the Stations of the Cross consistently impresses Jewish youth and adults with the centrality of suffering—and not love—as the major metaphor of Catholicism. Whether this is just an impression, or whether this impression is grounded in reality, is of little consequence. The learning experience is first-hand and intense.

The same is true of hearing Protestant ministers and laity speak of Christian theologies. Jewish listeners tend to marvel at the seemingly tortuous explanations Protestants evolve to deal with the problem of the simultaneous humanity and deity of Jesus. Again, whether this is merely a failure of Jews to comprehend the nature of the problems or an example of real theological pathos is not the issue. The fact remains that Jewish listeners tend to pose some challenging and difficult questions—questions which, regarding their source, cannot be satisfactorily answered. It is similarly reaffirming for Protestants to listen to explanations of Jewish theology—explanations which seldom satisfy their need to know why Jews cannot accept Jesus, who, after all, *was* a Jew.

It is appropriate to visit churches when studying comparative religion, Hellenism and Judaism, or the rabbinic period; and also when dealing with conflicting holidays such as Easter/Passover and Ḥanukkah/Christmas, and when confronting issues such as the quality of Jewish life in the diaspora, sin and the presence of evil, and so forth.

Visiting Libraries

Nearly every subject provides reason enough for leaving the classroom and visiting the library. When students have been divided into small groups to work on particular parts of projects, or when individuals have been assigned research, the library is a valuable asset. For young children, the library is an alternative to the story corner. A trained librarian willingly will prepare short "book talks" for students on almost any level—including adults. And, when no librarian is available, teachers can prepare book talks for their own students.

To prepare a book talk is an art akin to storytelling itself. But the purpose of a book talk is to induce students to choose this book or that to check out and read independently. So a good book talk tells just enough to tantalize. It sets the stage, but it does not complete the story. Some librarians include brief readings from the book as a part of the book talk (or, in the case of a book for early readers, display some of the pictures to the audience to give them a glimpse of the action); and teachers generally find it easier to prepare a book talk using this technique.

Perhaps the most important thing (aside from exuding passion for the books) is choosing books appropriate to the subject and appropriate for the students. Storytellers have the luxury of using a single story on many levels by "pitching" it to their audience. "Book talkers" do not have this luxury. The book is either age-appropriate or not.

If your synagogue or temple has no library—or has only a religious school library, or only an adult library—you can consider leaving the building once or twice during the year to visit the public library (which usually has a small selection of Jewish or Jewishly-related books). Alternatively, you may wish to consider asking everyone in the class to bring in books on the topic being studied. The books you gather can be made into a class library shelf to be used as reference or reading for pleasure.

The library is a recurrent theme in this book. It is, after all, the ultimate resource for literacy—whether it is the library of the student, the synagogue, the locality, or the teacher.

In this last regard, I have a word to say. Nothing strengthens a good teacher like a good teaching library. If there is not one available locally, you must build one for yourself. You can get a good start by choosing some of the books listed in the bibliography at the end of this book.

Of course, you will want to heed the advice of the unknown teacher who wrote:

"See the book. Isn't the book pretty? It is blue. It is a pro-fess-ion-al book. It would be good for teachers to read. I am not going to read it. I am going to read *People*. It has pretty pictures in it. There are funny stories in it. I make my pupils read ser-i-ous books. They must not read *People*."

Museum Visits

If there is a Jewish museum in your vicinity, you will need to plan ahead to visit it. Most Jewish museums find themselves swamped at peak visitation times—especially during the weeks of a traveling or special exhibit. Check to see that the school is on the mailing list of the museum. If it is, look at the calendar as far in advance as possible in order to book your visit date as early as possible.

If you are not near a Jewish museum, check the calendars of secular art, natural history, science, and other museums nearby for any shows which might (even dimly) relate to the subjects which you will be teaching. With a little research, you can always add a Jewish perspective to a secular exhibit.

Visiting Jewish Agencies

Most Jewish communities sponsor one or more of the many kinds of Jewish agencies. There may be a Federation, a Jewish Family Service, a Jewish hospital, a Jewish Home for the Aged, a Jewish service for the blind, perhaps even a soup kitchen partially sponsored by the Jewish community. When you are studying Jewish history, American Judaism, *tzedakah*, Jewish "helpers," Jewish civics, and Jewish ethics, visits to a community-sponsored agencies can provide much insight.

In a sense, too, every class is always studying *tzedakah*, since all classes participate in the widespread practice of giving *Keren Ami* (literally translated as "My People's Fund") at the start or close of sessions. At some point in every year it is important to pause and review the reasons for this practice. And there is no more beautiful way to conduct this review than by visiting one of the places the money helps to support.

Of course, one of the main things which the money goes to support is the State of Israel itself. It would be nice (but probably a pipe dream) to plan a class outing to Mount Scopus. There are, however, viable alternatives. You can import a speaker (if not from Israel, from the local Federation or from some agency in Israel), ask a parent to come in and talk about a recent trip to Israel (accompanied by videotape or slides, if possible), set up committees for correspondence early in the year to write to Israeli agencies and report to the class when they receive a reply, or arrange an Israel fair.

Staging and Attending Ceremonies

An interesting alternative to the field trip is a staged field trip. While it is sometimes possible to schedule a class to attend an actual naming, Bar/Bat Mitzvah, confirmation, wedding, consecration, or *hanukkat habayit* (dedication of a house and affixing of the *mezuzah*), it is usually an intrusion to the celebrants. However, you can gain the same benefits by staging these and many other ceremonies, or by attending rehearsals for the actual ceremonies. In studying prayer, Hebrew, life cycle, holidays, customs and ceremonies, and a dozen other aspects of the curriculum, seeing these ceremonies in operation leaves a lasting impression.

You already know a lot about this idea if you have participated in a model Seder around Passover time. The model Seder is a prime example of a staged "field" trip.

Interviewing Guests

Another alternative to the field trip is bringing in guests and guest speakers. This technique can be used in addition to the field trip, as well as in place of it. Some teachers feel that scheduling guests takes up too much of the class' valuable time. However, speakers need not be scheduled for an entire class period. Most guests would be delighted and not insulted to be asked to speak for no more than ten or twenty minutes followed by a brief question and answer period. You can judge for yourself how successful the speaker is and just when the class (and you) have had enough time with the speaker.

A few important considerations in utilizing guest speakers are worthy of mention. First, it is essential to plan the visit to fall in approximately the right place in the study of a subject. Speakers should not come from "left field," so to speak.

Second, it is important to let the speaker know in advance (and, preferably, in writing) exactly what is expected of him or her. This includes what the subject of the speech is to be, how long the talk should last, whether or not there will be questions from the class, whether he or she will be the only speaker during this lesson or unit, how the talk fits into the lesson or unit. Also, remember to add the exact date, time, and place, along with necessary driving directions, and directions for finding the right classroom in the building.

The rules for arranging for guests and using their services are set forth clearly in the text, but there is something more which should be emphasized here. The outside speaker can say things that you could also say, but which will have more effect coming from an outsider. If this is the case with a particular speaker you invite, do not *hope* that he or she will have these things ready to say, *make certain* by asking the speaker in advance to make certain points on your behalf. Most outside speakers know just how effective this can be and will be more than willing to cooperate with you in your effort to get an important point across.

Third, be certain to let the class know about the speaker in advance, including the topic of the talk. It is a good idea, too, to help the class prepare questions in advance. This will eliminate that most embarrassing of all classroom situations—the one where the speaker says, "Are there any questions?" and the class sits dumbfounded and overwhelmed.

Fourth, always ask the speaker for a proper resume. And always read it carefully before introducing the speaker. I use a highlighting pen to place emphasis on those items in the resume which are most important and most interesting to the group being addressed. These I read verbatim as they are written in the resume. Keep your introduction short and to the point, but cover everything that should be covered. The group needs a proper appreciation of the role of the guest speaker and the reason you have chosen to invite him or her into the classroom.

Fifth, do the speaker a favor by directing the question and answer period. Since you know your group, you can call on individuals by name. You can also field the questions to filter out long remarks from the serious questions. You need not be as politie as the speaker in dismissing "questions" that are not really questions.

Last, send a thank you note to your guest after the visit. If an honorarium has been agreed on, try to have it ready on the date of the talk. But send a thank you note afterward in any case.

If you follow these simple procedures, you will find many good speakers ready to work with you and your class. And your behavior will reflect well on the school or synagogue, too.

Using Collections

Collections can be divided into two sub-categories for our purposes. There are those collections which you initiate and those which already exist and upon which you can capitalize. Many people are inveterate collectors, and there is no telling what people will take it into their minds to collect. If you are alert when you encounter your students and others in the community, you will hear of collections of everything from rare prints and antique coins to rare books and autographed letters. Some of these collections will be Jewish in one way or another, others contain Jewish sidelights. Try to keep a note of any collections you hear about—and who the collector is—so that, when the time comes, you will be able to call upon these resources.

In the other category (collections you initiate) there are myriad possibilities depending on what you are studying. All students will be avid collectors for short periods of time, especially if they are able to utilize or show off their collections at the end in some way.

Here are a few examples of each of these categories:

Clippings

A very few people are already collectors of clippings from newspapers and magazines. These people usually collect only clippings on a particular issue or subject. If you are studying a related topic, you can ask them to prepare an illustrated talk working from their collection.

Alternatively, you can ask students to collect clippings from newspapers and magazines for a given period of time. Newspaper photos and clippings on Israel abound. The local Federation newsletter is a rich resource for clippings on other Jewish topics—local, national, and international.

Stamps and Coins

It is more difficult to ask students to collect stamps and coins for a short period of time. However, there are many people who do this already, and you can utilize them as natural resources. Collections may be more or less relevant to what you are studying. And, at times, you may "strike it rich."

In a former position, I was fortunate enough to locate a man who collected stamps and post cards related to the Holocaust. His collection was not only fascinating in itself, but emotionally moving, as well. And I was able to call upon his expertise on several occasions. Many more collectors specialize in Israeli stamps and coins; and some collections center on Jews who have been depicted in stamps and coins.

Photos

Family albums can teach a lot about Judaism. They often include photos of family celebrations such as Passover and Hanukkah. They sometimes include two or three generations of a family. They sometimes include family trips in which Jewish encounters have taken place.

Photos clipped from magazines are another temporary collection which students can easily compile in a short amount of time. Especially when students are divided into small groups for this purpose, the collections will proceed rapidly. Small groups can caption and catalog the photos

...Preachers and teachers preceded modern advertisers in the knowledge of the ways in which the visual image can affect us, whether we want it to or not. The succulent fruit, the seductive nude, the repellent caricature, the hair-raising horror can all play on our emotions and engage our attention. Nor is this arousal function of sights confined to definite images. Configurations of lines and colors have the potential to influence our emotions. We need only keep our eyes open to see how these potentialities of the visual media are used all around us, from the red danger signal to the way the decor of a restaurant may be calculated to create a certain "atmosphere." These very examples show ... the power of arousal of visual impressions...
—"The Visual Image" by E. H. Gombrich in *Scientific American* 227 (September 1972).

and put them into an appropriate framework for presentation. They can be incorporated in a notebook or album and placed on display at the end of a teaching unit.

Objects

Media relate to education productively by enhancing the learning process, by becoming part of an educational environment which is created to facilitate certain kinds of student growth.
—"The Magic Lantern: Metaphor for Humanism" by Bruce R. Joyce in *Media and Symbols.*

You can create a miniature "Jewish museum" in your classroom by asking students to bring in any Jewish objects they may have themselves collected. Be certain to label objects (I suggest you use ball-point pen on masking tape for this purpose, since masking tape is easily removed afterward) with the names of their owners. Assembling and labeling the exhibit can be a project of a small group or an entire class.

Genealogy

A unique form of "collecting" is genealogy. Those who are preparing family histories generally collect documents such as copies of birth certificates, town records, burial records, ship manifests, naturalization certificates, military discharge records, and the like. While these seem at first to relate to only one family, in the end it is clear that all of us are one large family, and all such records relate to us all. The more complete a genealogy is, and the further back it traces the history of a single family, the more interesting it becomes from a Jewish point of view. Parts of the history are no doubt anecdotal, and the stories throw light on general Jewish history. Other parts of the genealogy may relate to the kinds of professions which Jews practiced through the ages, where and when Jews lived in particular parts of the world, how and when Jews emigrated and immigrated, and how family destinies were shaped by historical events.

In this sense, the genealogist can provide both a collection and an armchair field trip. And it is fitting to close this chapter with this combination of the two subjects we have been discussing.

We have only scratched the surface of these topics, however. There are no limits to collecting and field tripping. It is left to your imagination and resourcefulness to see every possible opportunity for expanding your topic and your classroom.

Chapter 15
Study, Drill, and Games

In this chapter

The purpose of the techniques we have encountered so far is to extend and enhance your options as a teacher. Nothing is more to the point than to make drill and study more lively. Since a great deal of our time should be devoted to Jewish skills acquisition, nothing can replace drill and study as effective teaching tools. By including the last topic in the chapter—games—we are already pointing the way.

We are only now beginning to understand the physiology of learning. Almost two hundred years ago, Samuel Johnson said, "The true art of memory is the art of attention." To this day, his comment rings with truth. Hundreds of years before, the rabbis of the Talmud said, "The student who learns a lesson one hundred and one times is not to be compared with the student who learns it only one hundred times." Psychologist Douglas Hermann of Hamilton College suggest that rehearsal can be a potent key to learning. When you first learn something, rehearse it. Wait a few seconds and rehearse it again. Wait twice as long and rehearse it a third time. Then, after waiting twice as long again, rehearse it again. The "wait" periods make this technique more effective than simple repetitions, because you have to sustain attention.

Attention insures retention. And drill is the key to using this principle in the classroom.

There is no other form of study quite as potent as drill. But there is also no other form of study which can become so deadly boring in such a short span of time. For this reason, you need many options when you turn to drilling a subject or a skill.

Open Textbook tests

Preparing students for discussions involves drilling homework assignments. One simple way to do this is the open book test. Simply ask students to answer several questions with sentences, phrases, or definitions from the homework assignment. If there are students who come to class unprepared, this gives them a chance to skim the textbook rapidly. For those who come prepared, this gives them a chance to rehearse and refresh the lesson before it is discussed. This technique is also useful to the language teacher, since the questions set the proper emphasis for the lesson.

Hebrew Drills

Repetition is very important in learning. It has been estimated that to learn a given skill or concept bright children require eight to ten repetitions, average children 25 to 30 repetitions, and slower children 50 to 60 repetitions.
—Howard E. Blake, *Creating a Learning-Centered Classroom*, New York: Hart Publishing Co., Inc., 1977.

Hebrew reading is one place where using extensive drills can really pay off in a big way. But the drill of Hebrew reading should always be approached as fun rather than as a punitive measure. In the same way, Hebrew conversation classes can use normal conversations at the beginning of class to drill what is being studied. In both instances, the drill seeks to establish an element of comfort and an element of fluency. Many suggestions have already been given in the chapters on reading and oral work and need not be repeated here.

The teacher of prayer skills may wish to use a small-group technique for drilling. Students can be divided into pairs (*hevrutah*-style) or groups of three or more to rehearse the prayers being studied together before working with the teacher. The teacher is also free during this small group drill to visit the small groups individually and to listen to recitations in an informal and non-threatening atmosphere.

In the chapter on prayer techniques, we mentioned that prayer itself is a form of prayer skills drill. The in-class worship service can be an opportunity for effective drilling.

Dates, Places, People

Brief oral quizzes are a good method for drilling important dates, people, and places. If possible, the teacher should make a list (at the beginning of the course or unit) of data which is essential to understanding events, their history, chronology, and sequence. As the course continues, the teacher can progressively add new data to old for the purpose of the drill. The drill then should be repeated from time to time to help insure retention.

Map study drills

If location is an important part of the learning for a particular unit or lesson, students should practice working with maps. Individual students can be asked to locate places on an outline map drawn on the chalkboard. Small groups can pinpoint and label cities and zones on outline maps. Frequent repetition of map drills will enhance the students' ability to locate places and label maps.

Jewish Vocabulary Building

Making a dictionary of recurring Hebrew and Yiddish words and phrases is only the beginning of effective Jewish vocabulary work. Brief oral reviews of definitions can be accompanied by multiple choice quizzes and short-answer quizzes. Students can also be encouraged to use "target" words and phrases in the discussions.

Games

The game is a principal form of drill. There are many publications devoted to games and gaming in the classroom, and it would be impossible to select even generic games to present here. If you are looking for games to be used in the teaching of Hebrew or prayer, you will find nearly a hundred examples in the teacher's guides prepared by Behrman House for their various Hebrew series. Hundreds of noncompetitive games for teaching Jewish values and concepts are included in *The Jewish Experiential Book* by Bernard Reisman, and *Jewish Identity Games* by Richard Israel. When you use a game that works particularly well for you, make a note of it so that you will be able to use it again. If you do that, you will soon find yourself with a treasury of useful games for teaching.

Quiz Contests

Television shows and traditional games like charades provide another resource for games. Ready-made questions can be found in books like *The Jewish Information Quiz Book* by A. Kolatch and *The Jewish Trivia Book* by I. Shapolsky. You can apply the questions to formats like *Concentration*, *$25,000 Pyramid*, *Scrabble*, *Password*, and other popular game shows.

Workbooks

Many textbooks are accompanied by excellent workbooks. Some are accompanied by not-so-excellent workbooks. And, of course, some have no workbooks at all. If your particular text is equipped with a workbook, you may find that its best

...I am far from being unappreciative of the importance of diffusing [the knowledge of Hebrew] in the Diaspora...I see in this, first of all, a sort of "social cement," a bridge or social medium of contact between Jews in Israel and Jews abroad ... But if [the student] does not know to their deepest sounding, and in their context of spiritual tensions, such Hebrew expressions as *"mitzvah,"* *"averah," "geulah," "tikkun," "tum'ah," "yir'ah," "ahavah," tzedakah," "hesed," "mesirut nefesh," "kiddush hashem," "devekut," "teshuvah,"* he cannot carry a part in that choir that gives voice, consciously or not, to what I have called "the Jewish melody."
—Hayyim Greenberg, from an address given at the World Zionist Congress, August 1951.

use is as a drilling device in the classroom. It is not necessary to use all the activities in order to "get your money's worth." Use only those which actually enhance the class and lead to useful discussion or effective factual drills.

Worksheets

Worksheets based on workbooks can be teacher-made to use in drilling situations. They provide an excellent resource for students to use in memorization and reinforcement. Many commercial worksheets are available in the form of ditto masters and some are tied to specific texts, making their use even more natural.

Learning Centers

Creating learning centers in the classroom is an old-time art. Each learning center is a table or suitable cubby. Students can circulate through the learning centers in small groups or individually. Students can be assigned to complete one or more of the learning centers in a lesson or unit.

A learning center typically consists of a task or set of tasks which the students can accomplish virtually on their own. The teacher can check work as it is accomplished or between sessions.

For example, a learning center on Ethiopian Jewry might include a map project locating centers of Jewish population in Ethiopia (based on an encyclopedia article). There might also be a short-answer worksheet on the history of Ethiopian Jewry. There might be a copy of an Ethiopian Jewish folk story with space for a student to illustrate it. There could also be a letter written by one of the elders of the Ethiopian Jewish community on the present plight of Ethiopian Jewry, accompanied by a space in which students could write a reply. And so on. For young students, any one of these could be an entire learning center. For older children and adults these might all be a part of one learning center in a classroom unit on problems of world Jewry.

Learning centers are intensive drill stations. They do, however, require a great deal of advance preparation on the part of the teacher. Very few commercial materials are designed specifically for learning center use (although many commercial materials can be adapted for center activities).

To these examples of intensive drill work, we should add two more.

Suggestions for Creating Practical Learning Centers

1. Stay on the students' level. Consider their needs, their interests, and their abilities.
2. "Sell" the center. Make it visually exciting, make it invite curiosity, give it a snappy name.
3. Use your own talents—try to make some of the materials yourself. This gives an added personal dimension which no commercial materials can approach.
4. Seek out manipulative materials—objects and items which can be touched and pressed and pulled and squeezed. Such manipulatives aid in discovery and exploration.
5. Seek out related audiovisual materials—films, filmstrips, cassette tapes, etc.
6. Provide a broad range of levels in the activities in order to maintain the interest of a broad range of students.

Quotations

Judaism is a literary tradition. What it says is what it means, literally. Throughout the ages, students of Judaism have devoted themselves to learning what Judaism says almost verbatim. At first the Bible itself was passed down verbally, through memorization. Then the Midrash and Talmud underwent a similar process. And the process continues to this day.

Asking students to memorize important quotes is a way of continuing the process. And there is no subject of study in the entire realm of Jewish curriculum which does not come already fitted with a group of selected quotations worth memorizing.

As with the dates, people, and places that are important in Judaism, it is worthwhile for a teacher to keep a list of the central quotations to be drilled and memorized. You will find these quotations in many places, among them the *Encyclopaedia Judaica*, P. Birnbaum's *The Encyclopedia of Jewish Concepts* (Hebrew Publishing Co.), S. Glustrom's *The Language of Judaism* (Ktav), and R. Alcalay's *Words of the Wise* (Masada).

You can first introduce the quotations as key elements in class discussions, or by placing them on the chalkboard before class and referring to them during the discussion. You can ask students to record them in notebooks or quotation diaries. You can ask students directly to memorize them or refer to them so often that they become a natural part of the class environment. Like the dates, people, and places central to a subject—and like the vocabulary of a language—they should also be tested on a constant basis.

Flash cards

Just as quotations are one more form for drill, so are flash cards. Commercially prepared flash cards exist mainly for Hebrew language and Hebrew prayer teaching, but flash card use should not be restricted to Hebrew teaching alone. Quotations, basic vocabulary terms, people, places, and dates all lend themselves to flash card drills. Students can make their own flash cards to help them in test preparations. They can be assigned to work with these flash cards in pairs or in small groups. Likewise, teachers can make flash cards for classroom use.

7. Keep in mind that the tasks should meet the criteria for good motivation. They should allow for student creativity and involvement, they should make room for some student interaction, and they should be within the students' comfort zone.
8. Be absolutely certain that the directions are clear.
9. If at all possible, try to provide an answer-key on the spot. Learning centers are not meant to be examinations.

HOW MEMORY WORKS

...Experiments have demonstrated that certain kinds of review are far more helpful than others. First of all, psychologists say, the review sessions should begin shortly after the chapter is finished or the theorem studied since people tend to forget most rapidly soon after the initial exposure to the material. Second, frequent review periods, even though short, will fix the matter to be learned far more effectively in long-term memory than infrequent but lengthy cramming sessions....

The utility of frequent review as an aid to memorization is underlined by the power of what psychologists call "relearning"—it is far easier to learn and remember material that has been partially learned before. Familiarity breeds retention.
—Lee Edson, *How We Learn*, (New York: Time-Life Books, 1975).

To understand exactly how important drill can be, let's turn aside for a moment to see what we do know at present about the process of learning. The search for an explanation of human memory is being conducted along two lines. On one path, psychologists are seeking to explain how memory is stored, organized, and accessed. On the other path, neurobiologists are seeking to explain how the human mind can store something near 100 trillion bits of information when computers (even the most advanced) can store only a few billion. The work of the neurobiologists is made more difficult by the fact that, despite our enormous capacity for memory, we somehow manage to forget a great deal of what we store. Any explanation which manages to make sense of our enormous storage capacities must also make sense of our proclivity to forget.

Today—and I emphasize that this is a present state of affairs, and may have changed even before you read this—psychologists believe they have isolated two forms of memory in human beings. One form is *short-term memory*, temporary storage for names, images, and events. The other form is *skills memory* (sometimes referred to as "procedural" memory), more permanent storage for recollections of how to do things. Victims of Alzheimer's disease show how these two may be distinguished. The Alzheimer's patient may be able to remember how to eat, but not what was eaten; or may remember how to speak without being able to remember what he or she said in a given conversation. This indicates the division of the memory into its two components.

In short-term memory, our average capacity allows us to keep in mind (at any one time) between five and nine bits of information. (A bit of information could be a word or a number or even an associated phrase—so this allotment is just about right for a telephone number or zip code). Short-term memory can last for a moment (just long enough to dial a telephone) or for an hour or two (if it is rehearsed). Long-term memory or skills memory can last a lifetime. Once learned skills are not quickly forgotten. And once learned (even incorrectly) skills are difficult to unlearn. For this reason, a person who learns to type by hunting and pecking can become a fast and accurate typist. But once one has learned the hunt and peck method, any attempt to learn the touch method will cause a major setback in speed and in accuracy. Or, to give a Jewish example, consider candle lighting on Shabbat eve. Nothing in the tradition of

Judaism prohibits the use of a butane lighter to ignite the candles. Yet, after practicing the "skill" of candle lighting for many years with matches, a Jewish woman may feel uncomfortable and inept lighting the Sabbath candles with anything but matches, despite the fact that the match method is much more troublesome and produces a wasted match that must be disposed of in some way.

Long-term memory is more than just a skills memory. It includes experiences and events, people and places, dates and data as well. And long-term memory seems to be organized and accessed in the human mind according to subject matters. For this purpose, an emotion, a smell, a sight, a sound, or a touch may be considered "subjects." Any of these can access a whole series of memories in long-term storage. The smell of ḥallah baking may evoke childhood memories of a grandmother making *ḥallah*, may provide a distinct vision of a kitchen in a residence long forgotten, may remind one of the touch of a father or mother associated with the Sabbath blessing of children, and so on. Remembrances stored in long-term memory tend to be accessed in chains of association.

Some psychologists additionally believe that we recall certain long-term memories particularly well because we constantly rehearse them. For this reason, we remember many "firsts"—the first time we kissed, our first dates, our Bar or Bat Mitzvah, our senior prom. And these memories may seem more vivid to us than even yesterday's supper.

For our purposes, it is less important to understand what the neurobiologists have discovered. Nevertheless, in the interest of being evenhanded, and because it might help us better to remember the lessons taught by memory studies, here is a brief description of some of their findings.

The brain consists of nearly 100 billion neurons. There are more neurons in the average human brain than there are stars in the galaxy. Neurobiologists are just beginning to be able to trace the changes that take place in these neurons as memory is acquired. And one thing they have determined is that the hippocampus (a structure extending in an S-shape into both hemispheres of the brain) acts as a giant switchboard, directing memories to appropriate places in the cortex (the wrinkled outer surface of the brain) and the cerebellum (a structure at the back of the brain which resembles a cauliflower). It has been known for some time that the hippocampus also has strong associations with human emotions, and this fact added to the new knowledge of the function of the hippocampus serves to explain why

The intent of the learner is a clue to distinguishing between rote and meaningful learning. If the learner tries to make sense out of the material, meaningful learning is more likely to occur. A good strategy for forestalling rote learning is to have the learner constantly rephrase new ideas in his own words, forcing him to determine the substance of the new knowledge. One of the dangers of studying lecture notes verbatim is that the learner often [mistakenly] convinces himself that he understands the material. When the instructor's question places the material in a different context, the learner may have difficulty responding to the question.
— Myron H. Dembo, *Teaching for Learning.*

emotions and memories seem so inextricably linked. We can easily understand how a smell can evoke a chain of associations. It is still not understood how you will remember all the things you have read in this book so far. But, of course, you will ... somehow.

There is a whole lot more. Somehow, memories are stored along paths that branch out like trees, with each memory being a trunk or a branch or a twig or a leaf. These trees are electrical in nature, and connect through brain features called synapses which are somehow altered by the memory they contain. Just as mysteriously, the hippocampus knows where to place the next branch or twig or leaf, and how to find a piece of memory by tracing its path through the backwaters of the brain. The real problem for the neurobiologists is that none of this explains why we remember some things and forget others. We also do not know how much of our ability to remember (and the basic map of memory itself) may be contained in genes which we pass on from generation to generation.

One thing is clear in all this. Skills and procedures—and data learned in emotionally charged experiences—are almost always destined for long-term retention. And rehearsal may be one of the few ways to really insure that learning sticks. Drill is therefore more than a way to learn a thing well—it is also the best technique we have at present to implant a learning forever.

Chapter 16
Bits & Pieces of Odds & Ends

In this chapter

Classroom activities come in all shapes and sizes. This chapter contains those that do not readily fit into the categories of the preceding chapters. Some, strictly speaking, are not even activities—they are classroom resources.

Videotapes and Films

The rental of films from film libraries used to be an administrative chore of major proportions. It required cooperation and coordination, and involved advance planning and scheduling. All of this is still true of 16mm films. But the world has changed with the advent of the videotape.

At the moment, most videotapes are feature-length films. In time, the short films ("shorts") which are the most useful in classroom teaching will, no doubt, be available in local videotape rental shops. In the meantime, the teacher must continue to endure the inconveniences of scheduling a film in advance, renting it (or asking the school administration to rent it), praying that it will arrive in time, previewing it before showing it to the class (if it is new to the teacher), and returning it following the showing.

Because of all this trouble—and the expense of rentals—many teachers hardly avail themselves of films at all. This is a pity. Short subjects are often the perfect spark for classroom discussions in the social studies, in ethics, in customs and ceremonies, and in other areas of the curriculum.

The best procedure is to leaf through a collection of film library catalogs at least once—at the beginning of each year. Make notes of those films which might benefit your teaching plan. Narrow down the selection by budget and time. Finally, indicate the dates you will need the films and request them at the beginning of the school year. Going through the process in this way will make it relatively painless.

The Pros and Cons of Film Use in the Classroom

As a child of the new age...I am *naturally* hypersensitive to the phenomenon of vision. I have come to understand that all language is but substitute vision... The world's not a stage, it's a TV documentary.
—Gene Youngblood, *Expanded Cinema*, (New York: E. P. Dutton & Co., 1970).

Film "to teach through" can be administered, like mass injections, at the will of the school administrator. Unlike a book, which a student must read on his own, a film can be administered to hundreds and even thousands at a time in classrooms and assemblies. The only problem is getting the student to stay awake and hence the development and use of advertising commercial techniques—as in "Sesame Street"—that will keep his eyes glued to the screen.
—"The Uses of Film in Education and Communication" by Sol Wirth in *Media and Symbols*.

A few boards and bureaus of Jewish education have film libraries and videotapes. These collections are helpful because the job of selecting materials appropriate for the religious school has already been done by professionals, and the fees involved in usage tend to be minimal. For the most part, however, local collections are not extensive.

Filmstrips and Slide Shows

The school or bureau of Jewish education may also have collections of filmstrips and slide shows. The newest and finest of these come from the wonderful folks at Torah Aura Productions. Older filmstrips are of limited use. Some have sound tracks, some have scripts. Most have brief summaries and teaching suggestions. The procedure for selecting and using them is similar (though a bit simpler) to the procedure for using films and videotapes.

Some filmstrips and slide shows can be used as they are. Unfortunately, filmstrips and slide shows tend to date rapidly. Those which are produced in animation generally have the greatest life span. Changes in clothing, hairstyles, and other details cause photographs to seem old-fashioned five or six years after production.

Despite this, if a filmstrip relates to your topic, it is worth your while to preview it. Even if it is severely dated in general appearance, there are creative ways to use it. Among the visuals there may be a map, a portrait, a chart, a diagram, or some other wonderful visualization. You could turn off the lights long enough to show just this one strong image, ignoring the remainder of the filmstrip.

You can also view a filmstrip as a series of silent images, asking students to create a commentary based on their knowledge and speculation. Again, you can turn the creation of a new sound track or script into a wonderful classroom activity. In using a slide set in these ways, properly label any slide you use so they can be easily restored to their sequential positions after use.

A good filmstrip can provide an introduction to a new unit, a summary of a unit, or a set induction for a single lesson plan. The firlmstrips and slide sets published by Torah Aura invariably are accompanied by well-articulated classroom activities, which makes them doubly interesting in this category.

Teacher's Guides

Some people believe that being creative means going it on your own. I believe that human creativity means the reshaping and customizing of materials already extant and within our grasp. The trick of teaching genius is to combine the best possible materials in the most useful way. Reading a book does not destroy native creativity, it can spark imagination through suggestion.

The same is true for teacher's guides published as companions to the textbooks used in our schools. Some are done wonderfully well and some are demonstrably bad. But master teachers should not spurn the use of any teacher's guide. The authors of teaching materials spend a great deal of time concentrating on each lesson plan and example. Even if the guide is not immediately usable, its preparation usually shows through. It provides hints for every teacher, and it can provide the raw material the creative teacher needs to be truly inventive.

Cooking

We often make jokes about "dietary Jews," those whose Jewish identity consists of a love of kosher hot dogs, lox and bagels, knishes, and potato pancakes. Actually, a heritage of ethnic foods is a unique feature of most complex cultures, Judaism included. As with music, Jews have the added luxury of having adopted and adapted ethnic foods from nearly every land and people throughout the world. In addition, Israel has created a minor cuisine of its own, blending Near Eastern and European foods.

Jewish teachers can find many times during the year when cooking or serving a Jewish food is appropriate. This may be in conjunction with holiday celebrations, or as an adjunct to a particular course of study. Students love to cook together and love to consume what they have cooked.

In planning cooking for a class, keep in mind both the preparation time and the cooking time. Use simple recipes and minimize time usage as far as possible. Provide a copy of the recipe for every student as a handout, so that the recipe can be replicated at home.

A talented teacher I know provided this example of a simple and effective cooking lesson for young children: She brought in tubes of prepared biscuit dough from the grocery and divided the dough among the students. She showed the students how to divide their dough in half and roll it out and twist it into the shape of a *ḥallah*. Then she wrapped each of

...The packaging of course content is only one part of curriculum development and...even when dealing with an identical topic in a highly structured curriculum package, the actual course content will differ markedly according to the differences in teachers' instructional styles and perceptions of the subject matter. To some curriculum developers, such findings might be interpreted as pointing to the need to train teachers so that the subject matter is conveyed to the student more uniformly. But effective teaching is not mechanical. It is dependent on individual variation and the professional teacher's latitude in interpreting the subject matter and in effecting his own teaching style—since the teaching-learning process is not simply an established-convergent situation but is to a great extent an emergent situation.
—Tanner and Tanner, *Curriculum Development*.

the miniature breads in tin foil and sent it home along with cooking directions copied from the side of the biscuit package and a recipe for real *hallah*. The whole lesson took fifteen minutes—an elegant and eloquent fifteen minutes, that also extended the classroom's relevance into the home.

Transparencies and Overhead Projectors

The overhead projector is a flexible tool, and easy to use. You can use a series of transparencies or a single transparency. You can discuss the image while it is being projected or after. You can enhance a transparency with overlays or apply grease crayon or pointer to it while it is being projected. And you will find transparencies useful in explicating chronology, relationships, geography, trends, and movements. Transparencies are easily made (the students can make them) and easily stored.

Current and Special Events

Everything that is reported in the media is fodder for the classroom. But there is so much going on at any given moment that the problem is one of selection. In the early 1960s, the National Education Association suggested five criteria for selecting and presenting topical current events in the classroom:

Significance: Only significant issues, problems, and events—and only those which are on the students' level—should be selected for study. In general, ask yourself if the students you are working with are likely to have an opinion to offer. If so, the material is probably workable.

Point of View: Topical material should allow for more than one point of view. The points of view presented in the classroom should cover the range one is likely to encounter in the community. One of the values which teachers can promote through current events study is a healthy respect for other people's point of view.

Critical Thinking: Teachers should use methods which encourage critical thinking and open-mindedness. In most cases, teachers should try to avoid propagandizing any single point of view on a controversial issue. This means that teachers should try not to take sides on such issues. However, in dealing with Jewish issues in a Jewish religious school, a certain amount of latitude on this point should be allowed. Judaism often has something specific to say on an issue which is otherwise controversial. If it does, use quotations and citations to present Jewish points of view.

Data: Try not to speak "off the top of your head." Prepare before class and present the necessary background information, possible consequences of various actions, and any fallacies of thinking, logic, and argumentation you might find in the source from which you are working.

Flexibility: Stress the necessity for students to keep an open mind (and include yourself in this). That is, repeat frequently that it is permissible for people to change their minds based on new information.

If you follow these basic points, you will find that teaching current events will proceed easily.

Homework

In several other places we have spoken of specific activities involving homework. Most religious educators agree that homework should not be assigned for its own sake. There are times, however, when it is both relevant and meaningful, as, for example, when homework can extend the influence of the teacher and class into the parent-child relationship.

Having students take surveys on important issues is a sure way of involving home and family in the work of the school. It is also a brief homework assignment, and likely to come back done. And it points to a rule of thumb for homework: you should only assign homework that is likely to be done. Controlled success is an important aspect of all teaching activities, but it is the *most* important aspect of homework activities.

Tests

Testing is another subject which we have encountered many times before. There is a rule here, too: Tests do not tell you a great deal about what students have learned, but they do tell you a great deal about how effectively you have taught. If you keep this rule in mind, you will obtain a perspective from which tests can become useful not only in diagnosis, but as drill and activity as well.

Evaluations and Report Cards

Report cards and personal evaluations are times for communication with parents. They should reflect what the class has done, what you are planning to do in the future, and how the student fits into the class as a whole. They should also be personal, sharing insights and concerns. If it is likely that a student will be receiving a negative report card, it is important that the administrator or teacher be in contact with the family far enough in advance to give the student a chance to change.

The Standard Error of Measurement

Since Jewish teachers rarely have the benefit of standardized tests, the tendency is for all testing to be teacher-made. There is no reason why a teacher-made test should necessarily be better or worse than a standardized test, but in evaluation the Jewish teacher tends to forget that all tests contain what is known in the trade as "the standard error of measurement." That is, no test ever absolutely reflects what has been learned or what is known by the student. It is always a question of "plus-or-minus" a certain degree of testing accuracy, even if a test is limited to only what was actually taught in a particular unit by a particular teacher. This is even more true when it comes to report card grading. Just a reminder, then, to remain ever wary of that worm in every apple—"the standard error of measurement."

The better the teacher,
  the fairer the grade,
So therefore an interesting
  point can be made:
It seems only right
  (and a fabulous thought)
For pupils to mark on how
  teachers have taught.
—Posted on a wall in the teacher's lounge in a Great Neck, NY synagogue.

Creating a Classroom Democracy

Classroom democracy is a way of improving class solidarity and teaching cooperation at the same time. The basic idea is to elect a class president, vice-president, secretary, and treasurer, and to hold a formal ten-minute meeting each session or one half-hour meeting each month.

This notion of class democracy goes through phases of popularity. Up to the 1960s it was a standard feature in most public schools. During the disquietude of the Vietnam conflict, it dropped out of favor as the emphasis turned to "relevant action." Following Vietnam, the schools turned inward, leaving politics and "relevance to society" pretty much behind. The result was the "left-handed teaching revolution," sparked by values clarification, the rediscovery of the affective domain, and—in the final analysis—the abrogation of political responsibility.

Neil Postman, whose book *Teaching as a Subversive Activity* (1969) made him a guru of political and "relevant" teaching, recanted ten years later in a book entitled *Teaching as a Conserving Activity*. This latter book was neither as popular nor as influential as his earlier work. Too bad, too, because *Teaching as a Conserving Activity* is very relevant and very politically savvy in a low-key style.

Postman argues that the school and the community are tied together in a kind of symbiotic ecological relationship. When the community-at-large is shifted to the political right, schooling should liberalize; and when the community-at-large is in turmoil, schooling should seek to conserve the basics.

This "ecology of education" operates in a predominantly unconscious pendulum-swing. Postman argues that there are times when the pendulum is "out of synch," in need of adjustment. At these times, it becomes necessary to make the ecological process conscious.

Postman's book is full of fuzzy edges. Butetting aside criticisms for a moment, here is the underlying theme in Postman's argument: In a democracy, school and society serve one another. We, as teachers, have an obligation to the parents who organize the schools and bring the students to us. Parents—and teachers, as parents and members of society—have an obligation to the schools. And schools have an obligation to expose students to the democratic process.

The classic means to this end has always been the school or classroom democracy. The election procedures, the meetings, the voting on issues, the student court, the ad hoc student committees, and many other features of a democracy are illustrated in action.

Speaking of the ideal teacher and his role in the building of the democratic society, Dewey, the pragmatist, becomes a religious poet declaring that the teacher is "the prophet of the true God and the usherer in of the true kingdom of God." Because of this passionate affirmation of democracy as a means and an end in education, his friends and disciples maintain that what Thomas Jefferson was to political democracy, Dewey has been to democracy in education and society. This interest in democracy is also reflected in Jewish education....Dewey expresses the thought that should totalitarianism come to America, it would do so under the guise of protecting democracy from its enemies....Jewish education and similar expressions in America deserve encouragement because the survival of minority cultures is in itself a challenge to totalitarianism and anti-democratic forces.
—"John Dewey and Jewish Education" by Samuel M. Blumenfield in Judah Pilch and Meir Ben-Horin, eds., *Judaism and the Jewish School* (New York: Bloch Publishing Co., 1966).

Does this obligation extend to the Jewish religious school? There is good reason to believe that it does.

The Torah structures a government system which closely resembles democracy as it exists today. (Closely resembles it, but is not identical with it. For example, the basic unit of the Torah's structure is the family, not the individual. And, of course, the Torah is already socialistic in many aspects of government, while our democracy is only now moving slowly in that direction.)

The rabbis lived mainly under governments ruled directly or influenced heavily by Rome. They were naturally critical of governments and strongly recommended that Jews keep at a safe distance from rulers. These prevailing attitudes notwithstanding, they felt strongly about the necessity of good government. In *The Sayings of the Elders* (3:2), Rabbi Hanina is quoted: "Pray for the welfare of the government, since but for fear of it, people would swallow each other alive." In the Talmud, tractate Baba Kamma (113a), the basic Jewish model is made perfectly clear: "The law of the land is law." To this, the rabbis added, "A person must respect the government" (*Mekhilta, Bo*).

Working from these basics, as Jews have done throughout the ages, we can appraise the value of the classroom or school democracy in the Jewish religious school. What is at stake is our prophetic mission as Israel to be a "light unto the nations." Our task within the democratic system at large is to move our democracy ever closer to the ideals of justice, compassion, respect, and kindness—the teachings of Judaism. To do this, we must learn the democratic process and become effective at influencing it.

In a time when more and more Jewish children are being enrolled in day schools, the necessity for incorporating the democratic process into Jewish education is more important than ever.

In Summary

With this chapter, we close the unit on classroom activities. I have not attempted to cover the entire field. I am aware of some major omissions—for example, activities aimed directly at the learning disabled and the physically handicapped. Even in some of the material which I covered, I have barely scratched the surface. In all cases, omissions and deficiencies are indicative of my own limitations. I continue to struggle toward becoming a better and more diversified teacher, and I hope to continue to enhance my personal options in the classroom.

This unit is an attempt to expand awareness. The hallmark of master teaching is flexibility; and having a vocabulary of diversified activities means having options. Since students do not learn in one way only, all education is—to one degree or another—experimental. Some activities will work with most students, some will work with many students, and some will work with only a handful of students. As the teacher, you are the one who is closest to your students. It is up to you to judge what kinds of activities to use.

This is not a judgment which you should base on your present abilities, or even your natural proclivities. You should constantly expand your teaching horizons by trying out new activities and working with new resources all the time.

I hope that these activities have given you guidelines for developing your own options. You have the ability to use any or all of them. How you teach is merely a function of how you *choose* to teach.

Unit Three
Seeing the Way

In this unit

As it is written in the Siddur, "The end of a thing is in its beginning." In the first unit, we dealt with classroom management. The quality of education is dependent upon the quality of management. Teaching can only be effective in a place where learning can happen. The structure of the classroom, the behavior of the students, and the teacher's ability to control and manage all contribute to the ultimate quality of education.

In the second unit, we examined options—ways of making teaching more practicable and exciting, and resources for creativity and effectiveness.

I have not dealt extensively with the philosophy of education (despite the chapter on Martin Buber). My observation has been that, in the classroom, philosophy of education is a function of the teacher's own philosophy. Basically, I trust that philosophy develops and deepens in practice.

This unit includes two chapters and an "instant replay." The first chapter reveals what I call "the secret formula"—how to transform yourself into a master teacher. The second is my personal philosophy of Jewish education, given only as an example of how a philosophy can be born of practice. The "instant replay" is my way of reviewing and rehearsing some of the lessons I have learned and attempted to transmit.

Chapter 17
How to transform yourself into a Master Jewish Teacher: The Secret Revealed

In this chapter

Growth is not a function of aging. The aged can continue to grow. The young can cease to grow. There are sometimes factors beyond our control. But there are miracles, too. For a long time you can seem to be on the verge of new growth, but unable to move forward. Then, all at once, in a single flash of insight or action, growth begins anew. This is a moment of transformation. Suddenly, nothing stands in your way. A new freedom beckons, and you can respond without inhibition. This chapter reveals the secret.

The Primary Word

How can you transform yourself into a master teacher? The secret is in the primary word, "yourself." No one can transform you into a master teacher. You must transform yourself.

The basic tools are within you all the time. The fallacy is believing that they are "out there" somewhere—a great secret being guarded by just a chosen few. If you think that, you are not alone.

Henry Johnson of Columbia University's Teachers College tells a wonderful story in his autobiography, *The Other Side of Main Street*. He was teaching a class in methodology when a student eagerly inquired, "Dr. Johnson, what do you think the next method of teaching is going to be?"

A correct answer would have been that I did not know. But for some inexplicable reason a spirit of mischief seized me and spurred me to invention. Almost instantly I answered: "It will probably be the radiation method." Pens and pencils were immediately poised for taking notes on the radiation method. That was rather disconcerting, but having committed myself to the name, I simply had to supply a content. Exactly what it became I do not recall, but it seemed to pass unchallenged. After class I went to the faculty room and found there a visiting professor of psychology. Addressing him, I asked: "What do you think of the radiation method of teaching?" He reflected for a few seconds and then answered: "I think that it is a thoroughly sound method."

It always seems there ought to be a shortcut. We ought to know in advance how to achieve something we want and be able to achieve it in one fell swoop. There are times I stare at my word processor and wonder why it does not know what I want to say before I say it. Unfortunately, word processors do not write books, and teaching the principles of master teaching does not produce master teachers.

But you can *use* a word processor to create a book. And you can *use* the principles of master teaching to become a master teacher. The secret is that you must take the steps to transform yourself.

But look at this from another point of view. You *are* a teacher. You know how to teach others. Why not use the techniques and activities you already know to accomplish this feat of daring on yourself? Why not establish a curriculum for yourself? Why not assign yourself homework? Why not make your entire life a field trip? Why not collect the things you need, assemble and analyze the data, and make the necessary extrapolations to create new learnings for yourself? If you do these things, you will not only aspire to master teaching, you find yourself *being* a master teacher.

The Possibilities for Growth

Teaching Jewish children is a privilege. It is among a select few occupations which specialize in personal growth, in the realization of our full human and Jewish potential.

True, it is possible for a teacher to fall prey to unfavorable economic, social, or political conditions, even within the Jewish community. And teachers sometimes stagnate or feel trapped within the confines of a particular grade level or classroom subject. Nevertheless, the opportunity for growth beckons—dangling like the proverbial carrot. Natural curiosity and innate instinct can be regenerated. The urge to do what is right and what is just

The Jews of America have now reached "the parting of the ways." Within another generation we will be completely Americanized. The question, "to be or not to be," will then become even more acute than it is at present. There will be some who will find an answer to this question through complete assimilation. On the other hand, those who will desire to remain Jews must base that desire on the belief that a diaspora Judaism is possible. —"The School Man's Viewpoint" by Samson Benderly in *Jewish Education* 20:3 (Summer 1949).

remains. Even the worn-out, burned-out teacher finds it difficult to "unchoose" this profession. The quest can begin anew.

Much has to do with the built-in paradox of teaching/learning. According to Jewish tradition, the student teaches and the teacher studies. Student is teacher; and teacher is student. The classroom is like the medieval alchemist's laboratory. At any moment—in the wink of the mind's eye—lead may be transformed into golden elixir. Seen through Jewish eyes, the mundane becomes the extraordinary. Something precious happens in teaching: growth. Intoxication is a by-product both of excellent teaching and breakthroughs in learning. Something exciting happens in teaching: Ideas live.

We can state with some certainty how the brain, nervous system, muscles, larynx, tongue, palate, eardrum, eye, and other organs combine to receive or transmit information. But there is as yet no sufficient explanation of how ideas embedded in the physical tissue and emotional state of one human being are accurately translated and transferred to the physical tissue and emotional state of another human being. Something miraculous happens in teaching: Communication.

The Power of Teaching

It would be naive to deny that education has its dark side. Good and evil exist along a continuum. Teaching can have influence—purposeful or accidental—in either direction. Study can lead to indirection or to perfection.

In the classroom, egos may be battered or elated. In the classroom, the surrounding world may disrupt—becoming the source of suffering, to be endured; or enrich—becoming the raw material of enlightenment, to be examined. Opinions may be entertained or dismissed. Systems of belief may be tested or challenged. Prejudices may be fanned into bigotry or exposed and exploded. Great advances—scientific, religious, philosophical, academic, political—may be disseminated and imbibed; great setbacks may likewise be imparted and repeated. Evil regimes have had great teachers, just as the regimes of human progress have.

Overwhelmingly, the majority of teachers choose paths of truth, justice, and righteousness. Historically, their chains of tradition tend to remain relatively unbroken.

In school, it is the teacher and the principal and other school personnel with whom the child identifies. He always learns more from the teacher than from the curriculum; from the way the teacher acts, from sensing the teacher's own values, from the teacher's sensitivity to these values in responding to everything that goes on in the classroom, school, and community...
—Louis L. Ruffman, *Curriculum for the Congregational School* (New York: United Synagogue of America, Commission on Jewish Education, 1958).

...The teacher is obliged to focus the pupil's attention on natural phenomena, on the evolutionary forces of development, everywhere on every living being. The teacher is to find time here to imbue the child's heart with a comprehension of divine providence that maintains the functioning of each creature large and small by hidden and wondrous ways that manifest themselves in the evolutionary process. The teacher is duty-bound to emphasize that the source of creation cannot be reached by scientific study and research alone— unless it is coupled with an underlying belief in the Creator of all nature. Such study is to cause a yearning for the creator while appreciating the significance of His creations.
—Abraham Isaac Kook, *Curriculum of the Mizrahi Schools* (Jerusalem: Jewish Agency, 1932).

Consider the prophets who, taken together, comprise an unbroken chain of ethical teachings stretching over the course of nearly a millennium. Or the teachers of the Kabbalah—Judaism's mystics—who form an unbroken teaching tradition of nearly two thousand years!

Consider the yeshivot, of which the modern variety are a mere echo. The yeshivah tradition of Talmud study begins in the Talmud itself. The first redactions of the Mishnah, the Talmud's earliest form, were created by teachers such as Hillel and Akiba as textbooks for their disciples. And, closer to our own time, consider the teachers of Hasidism, the teachers of Musar—the Ethical Behavior movement founded by Rabbi Israel Salanter (1810-1883), and the chain of teaching represented by the two movements of modern liberal Judaism—Conservative and Reform.

Good and evil, and how teaching impinges on them, are not matters for philosophers alone. Every Jewish teacher expresses a philosophy, whether formally or incidentally. Every teacher distills the elements—fire, wind, water, and air—recreating the world in his or her own classroom. Every classroom is a microcosm of the universe.

What You Are Is What You Teach

The formula is simple: *What you are is what you teach*. Moreover, what you teach is what you study—all the time. The science teacher applies science to the ingredients printed on the side of a box of breakfast cereal. The economics teacher applies the laws of economics to the forces bringing these ingredients together. The language teacher naturally explores the origins of the names of the ingredients and the laws of construction and expression which enable us to make sense of what is written on the cereal box. And so on. Nothing physical or mental exists in the universe which cannot become the valid subject of the teacher. The only limitation is our ability to grasp and to impart.

...In our case teaching is inseparably bound up with doing....It is impossible to teach or to learn without living ... Either the teachings live in the life of a responsible human being, or they are not alive at all...
—"Hebrew Humanism" by Martin Buber in Will Herberg, ed., *The Writings of Martin Buber* (New York: World Publishing Co., 1956).

Every course of instruction must move confidently toward its end. It must go somewhere. It must have a forward thrust that can be traced and identified. It must progress.

To create that progress, the course must be prepared and formulated. The teacher must be a critical learner, eliminating what is unnecessary for the student. The teacher must gather a broad swathe of data and choose what is appropriate for the level and ability of the learner. And the teacher must consider—again through study and analysis—the proper arrangement of the presentation.

Likewise the student chooses what data will be permanently installed—that is, the student decides what is significant enough to learn.

We have come full circle. The teacher/student and the student/teacher are one. By nature, human beings seek growth, potential that can be realized, directions and paths that can be profitably traversed. Jews seek instruction— paths of righteousness, justice, and tzedakah. Instruction is one traditional translation for the Hebrew word, *Torah*.

What You Can Learn

In this book I attempt to achieve one small purpose: to make you master of your classroom. No doubt, this will be beyond my skill. But it will not be beyond yours. You will be able to take the ideas and methods outlined in this book into your classroom. You will be able to put them to use immediately. They will make sense because they are already present in one form or another within your natural resources.

How can this be? How can I be unable to fulfill my task, and yet able to give you the tools with which to fulfill yours? The same question is relevant to all teaching. It is a part of the mystery of teaching.

The student you instruct today may be prepared or preparing to teach you in ways more intense and indelible than you yourself are able to teach. Count on it happening. Count on it being unexpected. If you persevere long enough, you can certainly count on it.

All of education—theory, philosophy, and practice—can be summed up in this one goal: to help one student one time to reach deep inside, make one connection, and achieve what my teacher Raymond Israel used to call, one moment of "Aha!"

Chapter 18
A Personal Stance

In this chapter

What is Jewish teaching? The answer is something you will determine for yourself. Each Jewish teacher spends a lifetime seeking the answer. And, at the same time, through a lifetime of teaching, each Jewish teacher creates the answer anew. At times, I think I have found what it means; at other times, I know with great certainty that I am still searching for its meaning. In this chapter, I share a few basic observations.

Tzimtzum

In 1974, Eugene B. Borowitz contributed a seminal article to *Religious Education*. The article was titled "*Tzimtzum*: A Mystic Model for Contemporary Leadership." He argues that the secret to understanding our generation can be found in relationships of power. Even seemingly pure relationships reveal a political structure. Borowitz maintains that "our hope of accomplishment in most fields rests largely on how power is organized there or what can be done to change that arrangement."

Looking for a new model for contemporary leadership, Borowitz points to the mystic speculations of Isaac Luria of Tsfat (1534-1572). Luria spoke of God, but what he said can also inform us about ourselves. His teachings turn on the relations between God as creator and human beings as co-creators. Borowitz observes: "Luria's teaching about God is appealing because it makes man, quite literally, his co-creator. His teaching involves so complete a shift to human activism that scholars can even speak of God becoming passive in the process."

Before Luria it was supposed that creation is a process that takes place from the inside out. God expresses a will to create ("Let there be light..."), and the created thing comes into existence ("And there was light."). Luria begins instead with a question, "If God is everywhere, how can there be any place outside God for God to create in?" If this question seems too grounded in anthropomorphism, it can be

In the mystical model of the world, God's presence enters reality in stages, so as not to flood it. The intellectual presence of God in creation was represented by *Keter* (The Crown), *Hokhmah* (Wisdom), and *Binah* (Understanding)—with the later inclusion of *Da'at* (Knowledge) as the way The Crown appears in creation. The psychic presence was revealed through *Gedulah* (Greatness)—or, alternately, *Hesed* (Love); *Gevurah* (Strength)—or, alternately, *Din* (Justice); and *Tiferet* (Beauty)—or, alternately, *Rahamim* (Compassion). The natural presence was represented by the attributes of *Netzah* (Everlasting Endurance), *Hod* (Majesty), and *Yesod* (The Foundation). The tree was sometimes drawn as a person, to reiterate that each person is considered a universe. But, however drawn, it represents a vision of God's presence in the world which does not hinder, but supports, human presence.

restated in an ontological fashion. In Borowitz's words, "If God is fundamental being, fully realized, how can there be secondary being, that is, being only partially realized?"

Luria makes the bold assertion that creation begins with an act of contraction (*tzimtzum*). God voluntarily withdraws from a portion of reality in order to make room for God's creation. "By this act," Borowitz observes, God "leaves a void in which his creatures can come into being."

The act of withdrawal is not without cost. Something of God must remain behind in order for creation to be supported. Luria imagines this to be something like the oil or wine that remains even after we think we have emptied the jug.

The act of withdrawal is a necessary prelude to creation. It is followed by a positive externalized movement as God sends forth a beam of light into the void. From this light, all creation, as we know it, eventually takes shape.

> For Luria, then, creating is a twofold process, a contraction which leads to an expansion. More, it is a continuing double movement, for God continues the work of Creation each day, continuously, and hence all existence as we know it pulsates to the divine regression and egression. Here Luria's sense of time and the opportune moves in a mystic realm no fine-tuned atomic instrument can ever hope to clock.

But the greatest cost of God's voluntary withdrawal is not merely a space in which God is present in only a residual fashion, it is "a cosmic catastrophe." We can best sense the dimensions of this calamity in our present search for sufficiently durable containers to hold the enormous heat of plasma gases released in thermonuclear fusion. So Luria describes how the divine beam of created light enters the void and proceeds through various transformations. In the end, it produces "vessels" which come into existence as they are filled with the light. But God's light proves too powerful for some of these lesser vessels. They are shattered, resulting in a creation which is less than perfect. Evil abounds in a cosmos which God conceives as good.

The *shevirah*, the breaking of the vessels, is not a reason for pessimism in the Lurianic doctrine. Luria immediately turns it into an argument for the cosmic significance of humanity.

Creation is flawed, but not entirely. Since God's presence, however slight, remains in the world, the creation cannot merely be chaos. Instead, we see all around us the "shells" or "husks" of what God envisions—the shards of the vessels from which the kernels of God's light have escaped. But something of God's power still inhabits each shard. Luria thus speaks of all creation containing divine sparks. By lifting up (redeeming) these sparks, and by restoring them to their proper place in God's spiritual order, all things could become what they were intended to be. The act of restoring the sparks is termed *tikkun*.

What astonishes us here is Luria's bold insistence that *tikkun* is primarily humanity's work, not God's. In everything one faces, in every situation one finds oneself in, one should realize that there is a fallen spark of God's light waiting to be returned to its designated spiritual place. Hence, as people do the good moment by moment and give their acts of goodness a proper, inner, mystic intention...the shattered creation is brought into repair. The ailing cosmos is healed. The Messiah is brought near.

Jews do this work of *tikkun* through the practice of Jewish law and through concentrating proper intention in adhering to Jewish virtues. Luria argues that, if enough people spent enough time restoring creation to its perfect form, God would send the Messiah. In Borowitz's eloquent terms, "if people, by their acts, restored the creation to what God had hoped it would be, then all the benefits of [God's] gracious goodness would be available to them."

Thus the words "desire" and "learning" must be understood. He who fastens his desire exclusively to one thing in the Torah—so that day and night he thinks of nothing else—will surely attain to the highest and most amazing levels of the soul. Such a one needs no fasts and austerities. All depends on the steadfastness and intensity of his longing for Torah, which must be like one who longs for his beloved...
— Elijah de Vidas, *The Beginning of Wisdom* translated by Zalman M. Schachter in David Meltzer, ed., *The Secret Garden* (New York: The Seabury Press, 1976).

A Model for Teaching

This idea of God's withdrawal and creation can be translated into human terms. Borowitz speaks of a model for leadership in general, but here I will apply it specifically to a model for the teacher in the classroom. In our age of power, we tend to look up to the teacher who is creative, whose actions mold the classroom and bend it to the teacher's will. But Luria presents us with an alternative. Just as God's power must first be withdrawn to make room for creation, so too the teacher who wishes to initiate learning must first withdraw from power to make space for the student.

Consider the normal classroom. There are goals to be accomplished, courses of study to be covered. Yet the approach makes a great deal of difference to the student. Students resent feeling that a teacher is using them to accomplish the teacher's purposes. Students enjoy teachers who convey the feeling that they can grow as they labor with the teacher toward common ends. Thus, the ability to practice *tzimtzum* in the classroom shifts the teaching model from accomplishment-directed to person-fostering.

> Leaders, by their power, have a greater field of presence than most people do. When they move into a room they seem to fill the space around them. We say they radiate power. Hence the greater the people we meet the more reduced we feel ... So in the presence of the mighty we are silent and respectful ... Who we are is defined by what they think of us.

By contrast, the Lurianic model of teaching "has, as its first step, contraction." Teachers sometimes are so busy doing things for their students that they forget to leave room for the students to do things for themselves. Teachers tend to talk too much. Borowitz observes, "when they stop talking for a moment and ask for questions or honest comments, we don't believe them. We know if we stay quiet ... they will start talking again."

This approach does not call for a complete shift from dominance to abandonment. Withdrawing to make room for student growth should not become a teacher's excuse for indolence, for refusing to plan, for not providing resources, or for not making proper demands on the class. The contraction must be accompanied by a suitable expansion, a "letting in" of light.

> Leadership in the Lurianic style is particularly difficult, then, because it requires a continuing alternation of the application of our power. Now we hold back; now we act. To do either in the right way is difficult enough. To develop a sense of when to stop one and do the other and then reverse that in due turn, is to involve one in endless inner conflict.

Instead of being a transmitter of ideas formulated by others, [the teacher] must develop...an independent, searching mind....Let our children see us wrestling honestly and openly before them with our own problems as Jews. Let them sense our determination to wrest from our age-old Jewish tradition the meaning and relevance it must have for us and for mankind. Let them see that we deem it worthy of our rapt attention and critical concern.—Jack Cohen, *Jewish Education in a Democratic Society* (New York: Reconstructionist Press, 1964).

Borowitz offers an example in practice. Even if a teacher has made a lifetime study of a subject, it is important to listen to what students have to say. If the teacher does not allow minor inconsistencies to pass by unchallenged—if the teacher constantly interrupts the student—the student's sense of self-worth may inadvertently be destroyed. On the other hand, the teacher can only tolerate a certain degree of incompetence. The teacher must interrupt a student who is misinforming the class or making major misstatements that may contradict following information. "Danger lurks equally in action and inaction," Borowitz concludes. "And with all this, we cannot help but realize that our judgment to intervene may only be a power-grab while our decision to stay silent may really mean we are unwilling to take the responsibility for interrupting."

This example sheds light on the complex nature of the Lurianic model for teaching. It may cause a great deal of anxiety in the teacher. After all, most teachers tend to retreat—that is, to teach in ways which their teachers taught them. And few teachers of the past used as their model anything like this.

There also remains the possibility that through teaching in the Lurianic model, the learning accomplished will be blemished and imperfect, like the shattered vessels of creation. It is only logical that *tzimtzum* should lead to *shevirah*. Here, we have to trust that people can grow toward perfection, if we only allow them room. We must allow the students to do the work of *tikkun*, to restore our teachings in the course of time. It may be instructive to note that Luria himself used to emphasize to his students that they were all a part of one organism "and therefore needed to care and pray for each other." And, as for his own method of teaching, Luria proceeded by "hints and allusions." He did not talk too much.

...Jewish teachers...are insecure—as we all are—about our own Jewish identity. Why should we expect Jewish teachers to be any better at this than Jewish parents?
—"The Social Background of American Jewish Education" by Nathan Glazer in Nathan Glazer, ed., *Jewish Education and Jewish Identity* (New York: American Jewish Committee, 1972).

Seeking a Jewish Point of Departure

Since first reading the article by Borowitz, I have made this model of teaching by *tzimtzum* a regular part of my work. In the course of time, I have found more and more reason to support it. David Ausubel's experiments, which prove that short lectures punctuated by other forms of classroom activity are the most effective, taught me that not speaking to the entire class for long periods of time does not mean that I am not teaching. Jacob Kounin's work in classroom discipline taught me that being in front of the class is not the same thing as controlling the class. Benjamin Bloom's work in questioning taught me that the quality of answers is directly related to the quality of the questions and not to their quantity. And so on, through a myriad of practical and theoretical concerns and insights which I have tried to pass along in this book.

What I sought most of all—what proved most elusive—was a Jewish point of departure, something that distinguished Jewish teaching in particular. In the Lurianic model as interpreted by Borowitz I found a grounding for a

Jewish methodology, and a hint of where a Jewish philosophy of teaching might begin. But this is not the same as a Jewish philosophy of education.

I have already mentioned in another context one of the great theoreticians of modern Jewish education, Franz Rosenzweig. As a young man, Rosenzweig also wrestled with this problem, never resolving it. He did, however, rethink the issue of curriculum for his time and place. In a letter to Hermann Cohen, he wrote:

> We are concerned with [the student's] introduction into the "Jewish sphere" which is independent from, and even opposed to, his non-Jewish surroundings. Those Jews with whom we are dealing have abandoned the Jewish character of the home...and, therefore, for them, that "Jewish sphere" exists only in the synagogue .... Within [the synagogue's] narrow sphere everything desirable is included. To talk only of the literary documents: [Bible,] talmudic and rabbinic writings ... the works of the philosophers—but all this notwithstanding, the prayer book will forever remain the handbook and the sign post of historical Judaism. He to whom the prayerbook is not sealed more than understands the "essence of Judaism"; he possesses it as a portion of his inner life; he possesses a "Jewish world." He may possess a Jewish world, but he is surrounded by another one, the non-Jewish world. This fact cannot be changed, nor does the majority of those with whom we are concerned wish to change it; nevertheless, they wish to renew that Jewish world.
>
> ... of the language of Hebrew prayer we may state categorically: it cannot be translated. Therefore the transmission of literary documents will never suffice; the classroom must remain the anteroom leading to the synagogue and of participation in its service. An understanding of public worship and participation in its expression will make possible what is necessary for the continuation of Judaism: a Jewish world.

Rosenzweig was speaking of the German Jewish community at the time of the First World War. His letter was actually composed in the trenches, as he served in the German military. What he said had profound meaning in its time, but has to be recast in order for us to fully appreciate it.

For example, we may be a bit surprised at the centrality of the prayer book in Rosenzweig's conception. Today, we do not view the prayer book as anywhere near that essential to our Jewish ethos. But if we replace the prayer book with the factors which do tie us inextricably to our Judaism—namely, our combined heritage of synagogue and Federation life, our common concern for the State of Israel, and our mission to explain to ourselves and to the world the meaning of the Holocaust—we may begin to shape a new Jewish curriculum for our time and place, as Rosenzweig did for his. In these elements are a beginning for a philosophy of Jewish education in the diaspora.

But even these do not completely satisfy our needs. To them, we could profitably add the definition supplied by another modern Jewish educator, Rav Abraham Isaac Kook of Israel. In his book, *Orot HaTorah*, Kook wrote:

> The goal of Jewish education is to mold the child according to the fullest possible potentialities of his natural dispositions and inclinations. If *halakhah* [Jewish law] is not the child's strength, then try to interest him in *aggadah* [Jewish lore]. If he persists that this too is not according to his abilities—do not force the literary tradition upon him, for it will corrupt him if he rejects it instinctively. If the child leans toward the sciences or "general wisdom" [read: any useful field of human endeavor], good! Develop this side of his personality—but encourage him to set a permanent time to study Torah daily, for Torah is becoming with productive pursuits.

Taken together, Borowitz's Luria, Kook, and Rosenzweig bear a message worth heeding. There is a commonality which may at first seem dim, but is worth expanding.

More Mystical Insight

In the last chapter I spoke of the fragility of teaching. A good example may be had from before the Second World War. As Nazism was on the rise in Germany and Fascism in Europe, a congress of Freudian analysts posed the following dilemma: "Since our skills are devoted to helping a person become more fully adept at what he or she is about, should we help a Fascist to become a better Fascist?" The discussion was complex, but the answer was a disappointing "Yes."

Since whirl is king today, we are greatly concerned with asking "what" and "how." Our supreme object is to measure and master the world, rather than to understand it. The outcome of the present struggle unto death may depend upon our philosophy of history even more than upon the strength of our military weapons.
—"An Introduction to a Philosophy of History" by Levi A. Olan, *CCAR Journal* 5, April 1954.

There could hardly be a better example of the "secular desert" at work. In the end, the devotion of the analysts was not to traditional values, and not even to concern for the outcomes of their teachings, but to their methodologies, their theories. They abandoned responsibility for *what* was being taught, preferring to concentrate on the *ways* they had created to teach it.

Jewish educators reach outside the Jewish community for new methodologies. This is commendable. But when the focus of Jewish education is turned to finding ways to use these theories and to fitting religious concerns to these methods, the focus of Jewish education is perverted. The wasteland of secularism then invades the religious framework of our schools.

Instead, we must focus on how these methods can serve *our* purposes. The schema into which they fit must be a Jewish religious schema. As Rosenzweig points out, it must emanate from what Jews still view as their common heritage. As Kook points out, our heritage must take precedence over the secular forces, even for students who will never entirely understand it.

The Jewish mystical tradition may provide yet another insight into how this may best be accomplished. According to Kabbalah, the soul is divided into three components: *nefesh, ruach* and *neshamah*. The *nefesh* is that segment of the soul which we share with the animal and vegetable world. The *ruach*, is that part which distinguishes good from evil, and which is inhabited by the two inclinations—the inclination to do good, and the inclination to do evil. The *neshamah*, however, emanates directly from its Creator. It is the part of the human soul which recognizes the Divine Will.

In my book, *When a Jew Seeks Wisdom*, I rendered what I think is a functional definition of *neshamah* as "religious awareness." Religious awareness is the ability to discover what is sacred in the ordinary world. It is the ability to see what is possible in what already exists. It is the ability to sense the right action even when a law or *mitzvah* cannot be found to set a definitive precedent.

Reb Zusya of Hanipol, a leading Hasidic teacher, was stricken with blindness toward the end of his life. As we would expect, whenever tragedy strikes, the human begins to doubt and to question. "Would a merciful God allow this to happen?" "Why does God not put an end to the suffering of the righteous?" Such questions tend to be on the levels of *nefesh* and *ruach*. Overcoming tragedy without jeopardizing faith requires a deeper strength. In this spirit, Reb Zusya assigned himself the difficult task of finding a blessing where there seemed only a curse. Using his religious awareness to overcome the lesser forces of his soul, he offered up the prayer, "Thank You, O Lord, for making me blind so that I might perceive the inner light."

There is no law commanding one to thank God for personal tragedy. Any such law would be both cruel and bitter. And there is no commandment requiring us to accept whatever happens without anger, disappointment, or discouragement. But what Reb Zusya realized through his *neshamah* is that no blindness is as destructive as the blindness of the heart.

Because religious awareness is that segment of the soul directly attuned to the Divine, we read in Proverbs (20:27), "The *neshamah* of the human is the lamp of the Lord, searching all the inward parts."

Jewish Education

Our understanding of Jewish education extends from these points. Educating a student Jewishly is more than the education of the *nefesh* and the *ruach* in their concern with how the world operates and the distinctions between good and evil. Jewish education also includes the training of the *neshamah*, the development of religious awareness.

Judaism is rich with occasions for the exercise of religious awareness, applications which exist in the everyday boundaries of time, space, and mind. The ceremonies of Jewish life, for example, and the rituals of Jewish celebration are prime occasions. Not only is the birth of each Jewish child fundamentally tied to the coming of the Messiah, but the wedding ceremony itself is called *kiddushin*, or "making holy." One sense the special attention of the community present in such public religious events, just as one senses continually the benign Presence close at hand.

In the Passover *Haggadah* we are reminded of the verse from Exodus (13:8), "It is because of what the Lord did for me when I came forth out of Egypt." Understanding oneself as the emanation of all selves throughout history is exercise *par excellence* for the *neshamah*.

And, most brilliantly of all, the Sabbath shines as an example, a space in time made holy once each week, a foretaste of the World to Come.

We can train our students to exercise religious awareness in prayer. We can train them to seek religious awareness in action. By living a life based on the commandments of the Torah, Jews have constructed a path which turns constantly upon itself, in which each religious action stirs the religious awareness to another religious action. One good deed draws another in its wake.

By far the most practical application of teaching religious awareness is in study and commentary. The custom of studying the *Mishnah* in memory of the departed, for instance, derives from the fact that the Hebrew word *mishnah* is the Hebrew word *neshamah*—its letters merely rearranged!

Some Implications

This is not a philosophy of Jewish education, it is a hint of the direction in which such a philosophy must proceed. The classroom is not an adjunct to the synagogue, the federation, or any other institution. It is an adjunct to seeing the world Jewishly, to gaining a consistent and continuous religious awareness. It is a place for honing the *neshamah*. Every Jew, indeed *every* human being, has the necessary resources—*nefesh, ruach,* and *neshamah.* Many train only their *nefesh* and their *ruach,* and still manage to live useful lives. But the lucky ones, the ones who meet a master Jewish teacher, learn the value of religious awareness. For them, the world is no secular desert. It is a meeting ground for the human and the Divine. It is a place filled with holy sparks awaiting redemption. It is a place where human discussions are held "for the sake of Heaven." It is a place where blessings are recited for a glorious sunset.

Every time you teach, you can bear this message. Every soul you touch, you can ignite. The power is yours to perform redemption if only you can withdraw yourself enough to make room for others to grow. And the real beauty of this understanding of Jewish teaching is that you will be learning, too. We are all a part of one organism. Is it too much to hope that we can pray for, care for, and teach one another?

Chapter 19
The Instant Replay

In this chapter

In a sense, this book has been a course of study, a curriculum for the achievement of a single goal. Throughout, the book has concentrated on the skills and attitudes necessary for master teaching. Now, in the final moments, let's have what the television sportscasters call an "instant replay." But, for our purposes, let's rearrange the subject matter into more memorable form.

Conceiving Education

Martin Buber's conception of education has played a central role in this volume. Basically, Buber posited that the teacher cannot instruct. The teacher can only provide a window on the universe, hoping that through mutuality (loving friendship) a bond will be formed that will encourage the student to learn. Education takes place all the time—the world educates. But formal education has special tasks: (a) to provide opportunities for the student to *originate*, and (b) to provide opportunities for the student to *originate in groups*. Education relies on the student's need to emulate God through creation.

Franz Rosenzweig and Rav Kook bring us to a closer understanding of Jewish education. Rosenzweig says that the student possesses a Jewish world, but does not have the keys to unlock this possession. He suggests that it is our job as educators to provide students with Jewish literacy. Kook points out that not every student will become a rabbi—that the end of Jewish education is not necessarily to create scholars. Every student can benefit from Jewish education nonetheless, since no matter what the student may become or do in life, there is a Jewish dimension in which the student can participate.

Isaac Luria developed a mystical theory of creation in which God and humanity together form a partnership. Eugene B. Borowitz extrapolates from this a model of leadership in which the teacher learns to withdraw in order to make room for the student to be active in the classroom.

How to Critique Jewish Schools

Among many other pursuits, the professional teacher will want a few guidelines on how to be a professional critic of Jewish religious schools. This tongue-in-cheek list will be a great boon to you as you prepare to write articles and books about Jewish education in America:

1. *Give yourself a title.* Many national organizations are quite willing to help you in this endeavor provided you have little or no previous training.
2. *Find some fault with the religious school.* Avoid visiting classrooms as this may provide conflicting evidence and cramp your style.
3. *Avoid the study of research in education.* Single instances are much more effective as a device for making your point; and, besides, research will often conflict with what you wish to say.
4. *Do not mention different (differing) goals.* The fact that Jewish schools have adopted differing standards of their own is no reason to judge them by their own standards. Assume that only your ideal of the Jewish school is valid.

To these great thinkers, I added a hint of what might some day become a philosophy of Jewish education. In essence, Jewish education is concerned with developing in each and every student a religious awareness, a Jewish perspective on reality which can help the student to see the extraordinary in the mundane.

Learning Strategies

Throughout the book I have stressed that the students we instruct use more than one learning strategy. Because each student learns in a unique way, all education is—to a greater or lesser degree—experimental. To achieve the highest degree of effectiveness with a class, the teacher must meet the learning needs of all the students. This requires the development of options, a large number of varied techniques. Perhaps the most important of these, from the teacher's point of view, is developing visual activities and resources.

Checking whether learning has taken place can be done in many ways, too. The most effective is listening and looking for "reiteration," the student's repetition in his or her own words of what the teacher has been teaching.

Motivation

In motivating students, the best practice is to keep in mind the three basic learning needs—(a) the students' need to be active, (b) the students' need to socialize, and (c) the students' need to feel confident and secure. Any activity which meets all three of these needs will succeed in the classroom. Here, too, it is important to remember Borowitz's advice: students gain confidence and security when we allow them the *most* possible freedom in the classroom, when we entrust a great deal of the responsibility for learning directly to them.

Achieving Objectives

We need to recognize our successes. Doing so helps us as teachers to avoid burn-out. And we also need to help students recognize their successes. Students need to know when new learning has taken place. There are a few major guidelines to follow in this regard: First, programming the classroom is best done in small blocks of time (six to ten minute chunks, with only such activities as arts and crafts, singing, debate, and other student participatory structures allowed to run to a full twenty minutes or so). Second, lectures should be carefully organized and prepared. They should be short; and they should be followed by periods of more active learning. Third, new learning should be identified as such and carefully distinguished from what is already known. These are the lessons to be drawn from David Ausubel's work in lesson structure.

Evaluation

Developing skills in evaluation begins with recognizing the fact that all evaluation, first and foremost, is an indication of how effective the *teaching* has been. Tests should be designed to let the teacher know if the teaching has succeeded, or as opportunities for drilling new learning, or as a means of proving new mastery to the students. In the same way, grading is most effective when it is based on reward rather than punishment, when students themselves have a hand in determining it, and when its effects are balanced against the three basic learning needs.

Discipline and Classroom Control

Most discipline problems are teacher related. In seeking to change behaviors in the classroom, the quickest path and the path of least resistance is for the teacher to change his or her own behavior. In addition, Jacob Kounin gives us ten commandments which can help us to determine (a) when a specific problem is occurring, (b) the kind of change we wish to effect, and (c) the precise moment to intervene. Having a graduated plan for intervention is also very helpful, and such a plan is discussed in detail in Chapter Six.

Classroom Management

The basic rule in managing the classroom is that when something is not working, you must try *anything* else. The most effective means to good management is good communication—between the teacher and pupil, between the teacher and the administration, and between the teacher and the home. To achieve communication with the home, give regular homework assignments that cause the pupil to interact with his or her family, be certain parents know what the class is doing, and use positive report cards between formal reporting periods.

Being Relevant

Teachers never grow old, they simply forget how to ask questions. Find out where your students are coming from by asking them. If you forget, ask them again. Ask every class, not just your first. And keep asking them. Enter into their world, just as you expect them to want to enter into yours.

5. *Blame all religious school weaknesses on a single cause.* It is best to find a lurking "devil." For example, the textbook makes a good devil. Dig it up and hang it every few years. Or, better yet, choose an anonymous group such as professional educators, administrators, or consultants.

6. *Do not provide alternatives.* The first and foremost trap which a critic must eschew is the trap of suggesting what might be done to correct a situation. If pressed, suggest something generally unfamiliar to the group. Try, "The National [fill-in-the-blank] Curriculum" or "The Radiation Theory of Education."

7. *Write primarily for the popular press.* Not only will you gain a wider following, but you will not often have to defend what you write.

8. *Remain aloof.* Do not participate in conventions unless you are invited to be a keynote speaker. And, if you are, attend only long enough to make the speech and eat a good dinner. Do not join organizations which may tend to take action. You will find a great selection of organizations which do not.

9. *Point out that attempting to reach a conclusion is only a futile "quest for certainty."* The back-up statement is merely

that doubt and indecision promote true growth.
10. *Always refer to the "good old days" in the shtetl. There never were any problems in Jewish education there.*

Listen to the music they listen to. Watch the television shows they watch. Read the books and magazines they read. And refer to all these experiences in the teaching that you do. This is the entire lesson on relevance: *Anything you teach will be relevant to your students, but only if you yourself are relevant to them.*

Master Teaching

To achieve the level of "master teacher," you must be flexible. Though each person's ultimate style of teaching is personal, it is still important to be able to utilize more than one style, to change styles to meet the needs of students, to utilize all your natural resources effectively, and to continually experiment with new and different options. Just as with the students, the motivated teacher is the one who is constantly *originating*. Above all, have no tolerance for anything that is boring. There is no subject matter which cannot be made interesting, and no class which cannot be made to respond on some positive level.

Teaching is a gift. This is not to say that it is important because only a few of us can teach. That is not the truth. The truth is that everyone teaches, consciously or unconsciously, all the time. But when the master teacher teaches, it is with full awareness. We teach because we know we have something important to offer—we are givers. The problem always has been, and always will remain, to find the right gift wrapping. The more choices and options you have available to you, the more likely it is that you will wrap this great gift in such a way that the students will be unable to resist the temptation to tear it open and treasure it for its own sake. Just as you probably remember one or two special teachers who made a real difference in your life, your students will find, when they unwrap your gift, that you have given of yourself. And they will remember you.

Chapter 20
Resources for Further Study

About this list

I have tried to keep this list to books for the simple reason that books tend to be easily available while articles in periodicals take time and effort to acquire. As you will see, some articles proved rather indispensable and cried out for inclusion.

I was amazed when I completed the list. Nearly everything I consulted was published before 1980! At first I thought perhaps I was losing my "relevance," failing somehow to keep up with my field. So I pulled down the education books I have acquired, and tried to recall those borrowed from libraries, since 1980.

My analysis indicates that there was a spate of very practical publishing (in the wake of John Dewey's work) which lasted into the 1950s. Much of this was oriented to curriculum-building and philosophical inquiry into education. There was a corresponding flurry of practical publishing beginning around 1965 and ending as 1980 was ushered in. This was inspired by the political upheavals of the mid '60s and the values clarification movement which, in one form or another, entered on the scene in the late '60s, peaked around in the mid-to-late '70s, and continues to influence practical educational publications to the present. There may be a trend already present in newer publications, but I cannot put my finger on it.

The most exciting reading in education which I have done recently has been published in allied fields—particularly in anthropolgy, applied psychology, neurobiology, neurolinguistics, and semantics. Eventually, I expect much of this material to emerge in a new theoretical form in the field of education. But, in this regard, I refer you to the cautionary tale of Henry Johnson of Teachers College in Chapter Seventeen.

What is "BOOK"?

A new aid to rapid—almost magical—learning has come to our attention. Indications are that if it catches on, all the electronic gadgets now flooding our schools will be relegated to the junk-piles. The new device is known as *Built-in Orderly Organized Knowledge*. The makers called it generically by its initials, BOOK.

Many advantages are claimed over the old-style learning and teaching aids on which most people were brought up....It is made entirely without mechanical parts which might break down or require replacement.

Anyone can use BOOK, even children, and it fits comfortable into the hands...

The best periodicals to keep an eye on, if you are interest in emerging trends, are *Educational Leadership* and *The Phi Delta Kappan*. If you are interested in improving classroom management and acquiring new techniques, you will want to subscribe to *Learning* and *The Instructor*, and join the Association for Supervision and Curriculum Development in order to receive its ongoing publications.

If you want to keep current with Jewish education, you should join the Coalition for the Advancement of Jewish Education (CAJE), attend its annual conferences, and receive its many practical and exciting publications. You would also do well to read *The Pedagogic Reporter*, *Compass Magazine*, *Religious Education*, and the practical articles in *Jewish Education* and the *Melton Newsletter*. Because Jewish education is a comparatively small field, you should also peruse the catalogs of its major publishing companies. A handful of these attempt to be instructive as well as commercial. From a teacher's point of view, you have the most to gain by studying the yearly catalogs of the Union of American Hebrew Congregations and Behrman House Inc; and you can learn a tremendous amount about the preparation of instructional objectives from the catalog published annually by Torah Aura Productions.

American Library Association and National Education Association.*Standards for School Media Programs*. Chicago, IL and Washington, DC: ALA and NEA, 1969.

Guidance for teachers who deal with social issues and wish to use media resources.

Anderson, Yvonne. *Make Your Own Animated Movies*. Boston: Little, Brown, 1970.

Written by the Director of the Yellow Ball Workshop in Lexington, MA, this book deals with cartooning techniques that work with children from ages five to nineteen. I might add that the techniques are not too difficult for adults to master, either.

Ashton-Warner, S. *Teacher*. New York: Simon and Schuster, 1963.

Sylvia Ashton-Warner's book is a classic of humanistic education. It is filled with warmth and vitality, and well worth your time.

Aubertine, H.E. "An Experiment in the Set Induction Process and Its Application in Training," unpublished Ph.D. diss., Stanford University, 1964.

Every once in a while, and despite the best efforts of the dissertation committees throughout the land, a dissertation actually makes a significant contribution to its field. This was the case with Aubertine's work in set induction which is discussed in some detail in Chapter Five.

Ausubel, David P. *Educational Psychology: A Cognitive View.* New York: Holt, Rinehart and Winston, Inc., 1968.

Ausubel has done pioneering work in experimenting with forms of lectures and developing a theory on the use of "advance organizers." Though some of his articles have been more concise on particular points, this book tells all.

Bandura, Albert. *Principles of Behavior Modification.* New York: Holt, Rinehart and Winston, Inc., 1969.

For those who think that behavior modification is merely the manipulation of the child, this book will provide the contrary evidence. For those who use behavior modification techniques regularly, and without guilt, this book will provide some well-documented guidelines.

Bany, Mary A., and Lois V. Johnson. *Classroom Group Behavior.* New York: The Macmillan Co., 1964.

The dynamics of the classroom are at the heart of the entire issue of classroom management. Bany and Johnson survey the extant material and research.

Baxter, Bernice. *Teacher-Pupil Relationships.* New York: The Macmillan Company, 1941.

Although the style of this book dates it, the thinking and suggestions shine through as clearly now as they did in the '40s.

Bloom, Benjamin S., ed. *Taxonomy of Educational Objectives. Handbook I: Cognitive Domain.* New York: David McKay Co., Inc., 1956.

Bloom's taxonomies have become a legend for their thorough research and development. Don't let the word "taxonomy" scare you away. What Bloom and his co-authors have done is to lay out the many levels on which learning a subject takes place. You can use "reverse-engineering" to determine how effective your questioning of students really is, and whether you are helping students delve more deeply into a course through your questioning technique. For *Handbook II: The Affective Domain,* see below under Krathwohl.

Borowitz, Eugene B. "*Tzimtzum*: A Mystic Model for Contemporary Leadership," *Religious Education* April 1974.

In the text I called this a seminal article. As you can see by the lengthy discussion of it in chapter eighteen, I hold this article in high esteem. It is worth your while to look it up in your synagogue or public library and read it. You will also find strong educational themes in the many books which Borowitz has authored. I have been privileged to edit several of his works, and I have found each and every one instructive.

How does this revolutionary, unbelievably easy invention work? Basically BOOK consists only of a large number of paper sheets. These may run to hundreds where BOOK covers a lengthy data program....Each sheet of paper presents the user with a data sequence in the form of syllabified pictographic representation...No button need be pressed to move from one sheet to another, to open or close BOOK, or to operate it.

BOOK may be taken up at any time and used by merely opening it. Instantly, it presents data...the user may turn at will to any single sheet, moving backwards or forwards as he or she wishes...
—*Quote Magazine.*

Brophy, J.E. "Teacher Behavior and Its Effects," *Journal of Educational Psychology,* 71, 1979, pp. 733-750.

I receive constant challenges from wounded teachers when I tell them that most behavior problems in the classroom are teacher-behavior related. If you are among the disbelievers, read Brophy's study.

Brown, Dan. "The Language of Maps and How to Teach It," *Grade Teacher*, March 1968, pp.86-8.

This kind of down-to-earth teaching guidance is a great boon to every map lover. As far as I know, no book has yet appeared to replace this article.

Brown, George Isaac. *Human Teaching for Human Learning.* New York: Viking Press, 1971.

George Brown created a movement with his work on Confluent Education. The theory is sound—let's teach the whole child at once. The techniques were never well-articulated. The movement was short-lived. But there is an excellent teacher's diary in this book that makes the whole thing worthwhile.

Bruner, Jerome S. *Toward a Theory of Instruction.* Cambridge: Harvard University Press, 1966.

I find Bruner's theoretical work in education refreshing. Even as he moves toward the abstract principles of education, he always keeps his eye on the realities of the classroom.

Buber, Martin. *Between Man and Man.* New York: The Macmillan Co., 1965.

The only thing dated about this book is its title. It should be called "Between People." That criticism aside, this is one of the most essential pieces of reading on this list. True, Buber is a philosopher. But even philosophers agree that he is understandable.

Bush, Robert N.. *The Teacher-Pupil Relationship.* New York: Prentice-Hall, Inc., 1954.

Bush de-mystifies the human politics that run through teacher-pupil relationships. He gives plenty of background and all of it is suggestive.

Carlson, Elliott. *Learning Through Games.* Washington: Public Affairs Press, 1969.

There ought to be more books about gaming. Every one of them on this list is worth reading. Even if you do not develop games of your own, you will find hundreds of suggestions for them by checking books like Carlson's.

Castillo, Gloria A. *Left-Handed Teaching: Lessons in Affective Education.* New York: Praeger Publishers, 1974.

Gloria Castillo must be a dynamite teacher. There is a spectacular amount of creativity crammed into this little volume, all of it on using the senses to educate. You will have to adapt these activities for Jewish teaching, but this may very well be a mother lode.

Chomsky, William. *Teaching and Learning: An Introduction to Jewish Education.* New York: Jewish Education Committee Press, 1959.

Hey, this is the competition (to the book you are reading, I mean). What can I say? It is certainly more tightly organized than this book. It is a lot more formal. It has plenty to teach. Actually, I like it very much. The only drawback is that it is dated and does not benefit from the surge of growth in techniques and values teaching of the last twenty-five years.

Clark, Barbara. *Growing Up Gifted.* Columbus, OH: Merrill, 1979.

If you believe Clark, being gifted is a mixed blessing. But there are ways that teachers can help the gifted children in their classes. I have not included a chapter in this book on exceptional children (and the gifted normal fall into this catch-all category), and I am not making recommendations for reading materials on the learning disabled or handicapped. Clark's book, however, happens to be an exceptional book. Its meaning and methods really extend to the so-called normal classroom. And, in any case, speak to any Jewish parent, and you will discover that you have encountered the parent of a gifted child.

Cohen, Morris R.. *The Meaning of Human History.* LaSalle, IL: The Open Court Publishing Co., 1947.

All Jewish teachers teach history. It is axiomatic. This is one of a number of books which makes the teaching of history more interesting. After you read this, you will want to look at the works of Marc Bloch and J.H. Hexter.

Coleman, Hila. *Making Movies: Students' Films to Features.* New York: World, 1969.

If you are a Hollywood producer in Jewish educator's clothing, this book will bring you out of the closet and into the can (correct me if I am wrong, but I believe that's the Hollywood jargon for a film container). Coleman's work is filled with practical suggestions, guidelines, tips, warnings, and procedures. Whenever I see its spine on my shelf, I suddenly remember that idea I once had for a story line ... I wonder if Cecil heard that one?

Dale, Edgar. *Audio-Visual Methods in Teaching*. New York: Dryden Press, 1954.

Edgar Dale is widely regarded as a guru in the field of audio-visual methodology in the classroom. You will find this book extremely useful in developing your awareness of the available options in media.

Dembo, Myron H. *Teaching for Learning: Applying Educational Psychology in the Classroom*, 2nd ed. Glenview, IL: Scott, Foresman and Co., 1981.

I have regularly used this as my text of choice in formal education courses. It is basic and comprehensive at the same time, a rare combination. In addition, it is filled with practical applications, fascinating visuals, penetrating questions—and a good model for typesetting.

Dewey, John. *How We Think*. Boston: D.C. Heath and Company, 1910.

——*Logic: The Theory of Inquiry*. New York: Henry Holt and Company, 1938.

——*Moral Principles in Education*. New York: Houghton Mifflin Company, 1909.

——*The School and Society*. Chicago: The University of Chicago Press, 1915

John Dewey is the Dean of American Education. From his vast collection of published works, I select here only four which I think are essential for a Jewish teacher. I could have selected many more, but would you read them all? Let's compromise. You agree to read these four, and I will forego listing all of Dewey's work. That's a good bargain for you and a harder compromise for me because reading Dewey is a pleasure, an entertainment, and an education all in one. Start with *How We Think*.

Dunn, Rita, and Kenneth J. Dunn. *Teaching Students through Their Individual Learning Styles: A Practical Approach*. Reston, VA: Reston, 1978.

In this book I have only touched upon the subject of individual learning styles. Dunn and Dunn are able guides in this material and their approach really is practical and filled with good examples to follow.

Ejegelyan, Alice. "Introducing the Time-Line in Social Studies," *Grade Teacher*, Dec. 1969, pp. 76-7.

Nothing is as graphic and elucidating as a well-constructed time-line. And very few techniques which we use for teaching sequence and chronology are quite as flexible, either. Unfortunately, a whole book on time-lines would probably be overkill. Fortunately, this article deals with the subject. Unfortunately, though the article is the best I have yet seen, it is too short.

Elkins, Dov Peretz. *Clarifying Jewish Values*. Rochester: Growth Associates, 1977.

Elkins authored a number of books on values clarification with exercises adapted to use specifically in Jewish groups. This is the one I like the best.

Fein, Leonard, *et al.. Reform Is a Verb*. New York: Union of American Hebrew Congregations, 1972.

In the heyday of values clarification, the Reform movement prepared this offset publication mainly for in-house use. It contains many exercises which are specific to Reform Jewish history and thought, but most can be adapted for use with any Jewish group. Adapting these exercises, which are already Jewish in orientation, is easier than adapting those specifically designed for public schools.

Fisher, C.F., *et. al. Teaching Behaviors, Academic Learning Time and Student Achievement*. San Francisco, CA: Far West Laboratory, 1978.

Traditionally, educators have spoken in terms of class hours, computing an average of fifty minutes to each class hour. The study of Academic Learning Time shows that much less than fifty minutes of each hour is actually spent in learning. Much time is given over to "transitions" and "discipline interventions." This information leads us to the conclusion that the quality of classroom management may control not only the quality of teaching, but even its quantity. If you are interested in the details of the study, you will find them in this book.

Flynn, Elizabeth W., and John F. LaFaso. *Designs in Affective Education: A Teacher Resource Program for Junior and Senior High*. New York: Paulist Press, 1974.

Of this book, we might say *dayenu*, "it would have been enough!" It would have been enough if the authors had merely provided one hundred and twenty-six effective activities! It would have been enough if the authors had merely provided a beautiful structure for lesson planning (a model for any teacher)! It would have been enough if the authors had merely provided an excellent bibliography, but they also provided an excellent filmography and discography! And it would have been enough if the authors had merely provided a terrific index, but they also presented a structured thematic listing! We can all learn from Flynn and LaFaso!

Forte, Imogene, Mary Ann Pangle, and Robbie Tupa. *Cornering Creative Writing: Learning Centers, Games, Activities, and Ideas for the Elementary Classroom*. Nashville, TN: Incentive Publications, Inc., 1974.

The title of this volume should tell you all you need to know. It contains eighty-two excellent activities and games for inducing students in the elementary grades to write creatively, and some teacher strategies, too.

Forte, Imogene, and Joy Mackenzie. *Nooks, Crannies, and Corners: Learning Centers for Creative Classrooms*. Nashville, TN: Incentive Publications, Inc., 1972.

These two teachers really understand learning centers. You will, too, if you read this book. And you will also find that you can use learning centers in small ways—you do not have to turn your whole curriculum over to open schooling to benefit from this wonderful technique.

Friedman, Maurice S. *Martin Buber: The Life of Dialogue*. New York: Harper & Row, 1955.

Friedman's topical approach to Buber's life and work makes for a wonderful entree into Buber's philosophy and contains much material of relevance to Jewish teaching. He makes clear what many tend to muddle.

Gagne, Robert M. *Learning and Individual Differences*. Columbus, OH: Charles E. Merrill, 1966.

This is a serious work on individuation. If you have read Dunn and Dunn and wish to find out more about how your students map out their personal style of learning, you will be ready for this text.

Gamoran, Emanuel. *Changing Conceptions in Jewish Education*. New York: The Macmillan Company, 1924.

I confess: I did not really use this classic text in preparing my book. But I think some of you might be interested in the history of the Jewish teaching profession. If you are, this is an excellent place to start. You might also want to read Nathan Morris' book, *The Jewish School*, and the book of articles edited by Judah Pilch entitled *Judaism and the Jewish School*.

Glasser, William. *Schools Without Failure*. New York: Harper and Row, 1969.

Recent research indicates that teachers really control the amount of success or failure in their classrooms. Some teachers are actually failure-directed! That is to say, they unconsciously make the learning tasks they assign too difficult and their students naturally do not do well. Glasser argues for schools without failure—a conscious effort on the part of teachers to make learning a positive experience for students. This is worthwhile reading, especially if you think your students are somehow inadequate, or if you think they are missing skills which they should have acquired before they came to you.

Gordon, Alice. K. *Games for Growth: Educational Games in the Classroom*. Chicago: Science Research Associates, Inc., 1970.

This collection of games and essays on the theory of classroom games is one of the best of its kind. Many of these games can be readily adapted to teaching almost any Jewish subject.

Hall, J.F. *Psychology of Motivation*. Philadelphia: J. B. Lippincott Co., 1961.

Hall's book is a primer on the psychology of motivation. He covers several theories of motivation and compares and critiques them.

Harlow, H.F. "Motivation as a Factor in the Acquisition of New Responses," in *Current Theory and Research in Motivation: A Symposium*. Lincoln, NE: University of Nebraska Press, 1953.

This is a particularly succinct article. The title tells you specifically what it is. It will help you especially if you find a particular class difficult and need to change the way they respond to your course work. The rest of the book is also worthwhile.

Havinghurst, Robert J. *Developmental Tasks and Education*. New York: David McKay Co., Inc., 1952.

One way of conceiving of your lesson planning is to break it down into a series of tasks. Havinghurst is one of several theoreticians who deal with such developmental tasks, and his book is outstanding. Recently, the Union of American Hebrew Congregations based an entire curriculum on developmental tasks. Reading that curriculum, one perceives the difficulty inherent in this approach immediately. The curriculum becomes so activity-oriented that it loses the perspective of course-oriented goals. Students who pass through a curriculum structured in this way will have a hard time identifying *what* they learned, and a harder time trying to apply the educational experiences designed so specifically for the classroom to the everyday world outside the classroom. Where developmental tasks are very useful is in teaching the specifics of a subject matter. Like arts and crafts, values clarification, drama, and gaming, developmental tasks are a technique for dealing with subject matter and should not be confused with subject matter itself.

Hawkinson, John, and Martha Faulhaber. *Music and Instruments for Children to Make*. Chicago, IL: Albert Whitman, 1969.

——*Rhythms, Music, and Instruments to Make*. Chicago, IL: Albert Whitman, 1970.

If you teach music, these two books are essential reading. You will glean an enormous amount of useful information, many practical examples, and activities which can be accomplished easily.

Highet, Gilbert. *The Art of Teaching*. New York: Alfred A. Knopf, 1950.

If Dewey is the Dean of American Educators, Gilbert Highet is the Master Teacher. This is must reading. I assign it to you as your homework for this course.

Hoffman, Banesh. *The Tyranny of Testing*. New York: Crowell-Collier, 1962.

Tests prove that we either teach well or teach poorly. They rarely prove much about the students' learning. Yet teachers regularly interpret them in ways which are just short of punitive, base major decisions on them, and use them as a basis for grading students. Since that is true, we should also understand the implications of testing. That is what Hoffman helps us to do.

Holt, John. *How Children Learn*. New York: Pitman Publishing Corp., 1967.

John Holt has written a number of excellent books about the education of American children. This one is particularly relevant to Jewish teaching. Since he happens to be an excellent writer, it is also easy and pleasurable reading.

Hook, Sidney. *Education for Modern Man*. New York: The Dial Press, 1946.

Hook deals with the large question facing all teachers: what should education accomplish? Because the question is answered in practical as well as philosophical terms, this is an appropriate book for those who want to look deeper into the theoretical basis for Jewish education.

Huizinga, Johan. *Homo Ludens: A Study of the Play Element in Culture*, trans. by R.F.C. Hull. New York: Roy Publishers, 1950.

Beware! This book could change the way you think about living. It will certainly help you to "lighten up" in the classroom. In fact, it may spur you to transform your class into an intellectual "playground."

Israel, Richard J.. *Jewish Identity Games: A How to Do It Book*. Washington: B'nai B'rith Hillel Foundation, 1978.

Like the book by Dov Peretz Elkins, this pamphlet is chock full of already adapted Jewish values clarification exercises.

Johnson, Lois V., and Mary A. Bany. *Classroom Management: Theory and Skill Training*. New York: Macmillan Co., 1970.

As with their book on the dynamics of the classroom group (see *Bany* above), the authors here deftly survey the field. In this case, it is the field of classroom management. The book provides many useful examples which can help you extend your prowess in the classroom.

Kohl, Herbert. *Math, Writing and Games in the Open Classroom*. N.Y.: A New York Review Book, 1974.

Herbert Kohl is a master teacher who is also a great writer. This book is loaded both with good classroom games and more importantly with the descriptions of classrooms in which they worked. This is the book which shows you how to really use games.

Kounin, Jacob S. *Discipline and Classroom Management*. New York: Holt, Rinehart and Winston, Inc., 1970.
——, and P.V. Gump. *Discipline and Group Management in Classrooms*. New York: Holt, Rinehart and Winston, Inc., 1970.

Kounin and Gump provide structures for discipline in the classroom which are far and away the most helpful in the field. Reading these books will absolutely help you in your classroom management.

Krathwohl, David R., Benjamin S. Bloom, and Bertram B. Masia. *Taxonomy of Educational Objectives. Handbook II: Affective Domain*. New York: David McKay Co., Inc., 1964.

For the use of this material, see the description above of Bloom's work in taxonomies of education.

Langer, Suzanne. *Philosophy in a New Key*. Cambridge: Harvard University Press, 1942.

Langer speaks of art and the arts. She tells how the arts influence and educate us—intellectually and emotionally. This is high-class material, excellent reading for the serious student of art in education.

Lemlech, Johanna K. *Classroom Management*. New York: Harper and Row, 1979.

Lemlech's book is a straightforward examination of the theories and techniques of classroom management. It is a good set induction for more specific books, or a nice summary for those who have read more specific books.

Lidstone, John, and Don McIntosh. *Children as Film Makers.* New York: Van Nostrand Reinhold, 1970.

This is a description of the practical steps necessary for carrying out a filmmaking project with students. You can certainly adapt everything in it to Jewish education. The emphasis, however, must be changed: the emphasis here is too much on the art of filmmaking for its own sake.

Madden, Ward. *Religious Values in Education.* New York: Harper and Brothers, 1951.

For a general discussion on the place of religion in education, Madden's book is an useful point of departure.

Mager, Robert F. *Preparing Instructional Objectives*, 2nd ed. Belmont, CA: Fearon, 1975.

This is a programmed textbook for those of us who think turning to the next page sometimes gets boring. It is a pithy and brief book which has only one purpose: to teach us how to phrase an educational objective properly. I like this book. It really does what it sets out to do. If you try it, you will probably like it, too.

Maslow, Abraham H., ed. *Motivation and Personality.* New York: Harper & Row, 1945.
——"Needs," *Psychological Review*, 50. New York: 1943.

Maslow's text is one of the classics of the field of motivation. There have been many advances since his time, but none of them has managed to eclipse the value of this volume. Likewise, his article on human needs provides an invaluable point of departure.

Meyers, Lawrence, ed. *Teaching in the Jewish Religious School.* Experimental Edition. Department of Teacher Education. New York: Union of American Hebrew Congregations, 1967.

There may be a subtle message in this entry. For one thing, no edition except the "Experimental Edition" of this excellent text was ever published. For another thing, the Department of Teacher Education at the UAHC no longer exists. It seems that the Department turned out to be "experimental" while the text turned out to be useful. In any case, among many other gems, this book includes the "Summary List of Activities for Planning Lessons or Units" by Toby K. Kurzband which formed the basis for my own list of activities given in the chapters in unit two. Toby K. Kurzband was for many years the Educational Director of the Jewish Community Center of White Plains. He authored a manual for religious school administration and co-authored textbooks with Meyer Levin. Lawrence Meyers, who compiled this textbook for teacher training, made a significant contribution to our field.

Though the tone is definitely Reform, you will find articles and suggestions on nearly every aspect of teaching in the religious school.

Miller, Doris P., "Adventure in Educational Media: Making Sound Filmstrips," *English Journal*, Feb. 1968, pp. 223-7.

If making a film is too large a project for you, don't despair. You could be making a filmstrip—complete with sound. Miller's article will show the way.

National Council for the Social Studies, Thirty-Third Yearbook. *Skill Development in the Social Studies*. Washington: National Education Association, 1963.

This particular yearbook is a real winner. It is loaded with activities and examples and filled with practical advice on transmitting important skills to students.

National Society for the Study of Education, Thirty-Fifth Yearbook. *Music Education*. Bloomington, IL: Public School Publishing Co., 1936.

This yearbook is also a winner, especially since there is a definite lack of materials regarding music education in our preschool, elementary and secondary schools. Even here, the bias is toward theory. But there are enough activities to get you started nicely.

Page, E.B. "Teacher Comments and Student Motivation: A Seventy-Four Classroom Experiment in School Motivation," *Journal of Educational Psychology* 49, 1958, pp. 173-181.

If nothing else, this article describes the procedure for undertaking a massive research project. The subject, too, is fascinating; and it will leave you with many good ideas about how to improve your own communications skills in order to enhance student motivation.

Perkinson, Henry J. *The Possibilities of Error: An Approach to Education*. New York: David McKay Co., Inc., 1971.

Henry Perkinson is one of the finest teachers I have encountered. He teaches courses in the philosophy of education at New York University. This slim volume exposes a raw nerve in education. And it is a vital resource for good teaching. What Perkinson argues is that real learning takes place through error. Errors are not something to be hidden, they are the raw experiences which make growth possible. He proceeds to show how the ordinary error can be turned into a revelatory teaching opportunity. This book is a rare find. You will be gravely in error if you fail to read it.

Phenix, Philip H.. *Philosophy of Education*. New York: Holt, Rinehart and Winston, 1958.

You will better understand education as a profession when you have read a book or two on the philosophy of education. I recommend Phenix's work for this purpose. Although not all of it is useful to Jewish educators, Phenix does have a firm grip on the interrelationships among values, religion, and education.

Piaget, Jean. *Play, Dreams, and Imitation in Childhood*, trans. by C. Gattegno and F.M.Hodgson. London: Heinemann, 1951.
——*The Moral Judgment of the Child*. London: Kegan Paul, Trench, and Trubner, 1932.

Reading Piaget's work is stunning. It is difficult to remember that he worked in the confines of a comparatively small town with a few children. These two books, chosen from among the corpus of Piaget's work, relate specifically to themes developed in this book. Both are useful background material.

Postman, Neil. *Teaching as a Conserving Activity*. New York: Delacorte Press, 1979.
——, and Charles Weingartner. *Teaching as a Subversive Activity*. New York: Delacorte Press, 1969.

I have already spoken of both these books in the text. Of the two, I find the *Subversive Activity* book the most useful and inspiring. The other, which focusses on the "ecology of education," also contains some interesting facts about the influence of media on children.

Raths, Louis E., *et al. Values and Teaching*. Columbus: Charles Merrill, 1966.

This is the book which started the values clarification movement. Like most books that start a movement, its real value is intrinsic. You will find wonderful hints and tips on dealing with children in this volume, whether or not you are an adherent of values clarification in general.

Read, Herbert. *Education Through Art*. London: Faber and Faber, Ltd., 1943.

Read's book is the definitive practical statement on how art can influence education. It is beautifully written, too.

Reisman, Bernard. *The Jewish Experiential Book*. New York: Ktav, 1979.

This book is filled with wonderful activities based on solid cognitive materials. It is a rare find, especially because the activities in it are immediately useful with adults. The real pity is that we do so much adult education and have so little in the way of adult activity resources. In fact, adults have the same motivational needs as young people—and the first of these is the need to be active learners. I highly recommend Reisman's book.

Richardson, Elwyn S. *In the Early World*. New York: Pantheon, 1969.

Anyone who deals with early childhood education must read this book—or, at least, look at the pictures. Very young children are at a great disadvantage. They lack skills to communicate to adults an accurate picture of their world. Teachers must learn to be extremely sensitive to the many small ways in which this early world is revealed. Richardson makes this task explicit; and helps us to gain many valuable insights in a general way.

Rogers, Virginia M., and Marcella L. Kysilka, "Simulation Games: What and Why," *The Instructor*, March 1970, pp. 94-5.

There are whole books on simulation gaming which do not teach as much or as well as this little article. If you are adept at dreaming up situations, or if you are a true observer of everyday realities, this article can extend your aptitude right into a powerful gaming format.

Rossel, Seymour. *Mitzvah: The Teacher's Guide*. Chappaqua, NY: Rossel Books, 1982.

This teacher's guide was prepared to accompany the Bar/Bat Mitzvah text, *Mitzvah* by Jacob Neusner. It is a good source for teaching stories (given in italics and labeled "From the Tradition"). The teacher's guide also includes a strategy for dealing with questions regarding the existence of God (beginning on page 47), a classroom lesson on *anorexia nervosa* (page 51ff.), and a note regarding incest (page 81ff.). These are three difficult issues sometimes faced by Jewish teachers, and I hope this material will prove helpful. The guide opens with one of my favorite quotes about teaching—often given in a short form. This is the full quotation: "As a little wood can set light to a great tree, so young students sharpen the wits of great scholars. Hence Rabbi Hanina said, 'Much Torah have I learnt from my teachers, more from my colleagues, but from my students most of all.'"

——*When a Jew Seeks Wisdom: The Sayings of the Fathers*. New York: Behrman House, Inc., 1975.

Modesty prevents me from telling you that this book is worthwhile reading for any teacher in any Jewish school. Instead, I will tell you *why* it is worthwhile reading: In *Wisdom*, you will find stories from Jewish tradition arranged by topics like "patience," "love," "courage," "community," "possessions," "government," "sensitivity," "labor," and "peace." Exact citations for each story are provided, and an annotated glossary of sources is given at the end of the book. You can tell the stories in your classroom exactly as they are found, or, by tracing them back to their sources, you can discover additional stories on the same themes. In Chapter Six of *When A Jew Seeks Wisdom*, you will find the discussion of religious awareness referred to in Chapter 18 of this book.

Satir, Virginia. *Peoplemaking*. Palo Alto, CA: Science and Behavior Books, 1972.

Virginia Satir is a master therapist. She specializes in family therapy, and she writes about it lovingly. In *Peoplemaking*, she writes about education and what it can mean to the individual. Everything she writes is worth reading.

Schultz, Morton J. *The Teacher and the Overhead Projector*. Englewood Cliffs, NJ: Prentice-Hall, 1965.

Others might find it difficult to fill a whole volume with ideas for how to use one piece of machinery. For Schultz, it's a breeze. We get the feeling that he could go on for another couple of volumes, giving one good idea after another for making an overhead projector into a classroom tool. If you use the overhead projector now, this book will be like a good overlay, making things clearer. If you have never used the overhead projector, make way for a new skill.

Shaftel, G., and Fannie K. Shaftel, "Role Playing: The Problem Story." An Intergroup Education Pamphlet. National Conference of Christians and Jews, 1952.

I don't know if this little gem is still available. If it is, get it now. If it is not, try to locate a library copy. It really gives good background on the whole domain of role plays and impromptus. And, as you might expect of the source, it includes some role plays tailor-made for the Jewish (and non-Jewish) classroom.

Shumsky, Abraham, ed. *In Search of Teaching Style*. Englewood Cliffs, NJ: Prentice-Hall, Inc., 1968.

Abraham Shumsky is a good friend and a good author and editor. This book is very useful. One of the most important conclusions I have been able to draw from my teaching experience is that teachers must learn to communicate in many different ways in order to reach the many different kinds of students they face. Despite this, we must all develop a personal teaching style, uniquely our own. These are the twin concerns which Shumsky and the other authors in the book address.

Simon, Sidney, *et al*. *Values Clarification: A Handbook of Practical Strategies for Teachers and Students*. Minneapolis: Winston Press, 1973.

Raths and Simon put the values clarification movement into high gear with the publication of *Values and Teaching*. What they found was a crying need for practical activities that could be used in the classroom to develop personal awareness and raise personal consciousness on issues of moment to the community. In this book, the space allotted to theory dropped significantly, while the number of activities multiplied. Many can be adapted to Jewish situations. The danger here, like the danger with developmental tasks, is that students can quickly get an overdose of clarification activities. Try not to fall into this trap of "teaching" values clarification. Keep in mind that this is a technique for conveying more important materials, and not an end in itself.

Spolin, Viola. *Improvisation for the Theatre*. Evanston, IL: Northwestern University Press, 1974.

Spolin's book is intended for theater people, but the ideas can easily be adapted for the classroom. She gives many examples of how and when to use improvisation.

Taba, Hilda. *Curriculum Development: Theory and Practice*. New York: Harcourt Brace Jovanavich, Inc., 1962.

The subject of curriculum development covers a broad ground. It sometimes remains abstract and oblique—almost like the philosophy of education—and sometimes breathes the mortal air of technique and applications. Taba does a nice job of doing both. If you are ready to look at the big picture—not just your course, but how your course fits into the scheme of things—this book is a good place to start. So is the next one:

Tanner, Daniel and Laurel Tanner. *Curriculum Development: Theory into Practice*. New York: Macmillan Publishing Co., Inc., 1975.

In the field of curriculum development, Daniel and Laurel Tanner stand out as models. Their book is well-researched, rich in detail, highly organized, and well written. It is a shame that it was not designed in a more readable typeface, but that is my only gripe. If you want to learn about curriculum development—especially about the trends which control the schools today—this is the right book to read.

Tauben, Carol, and Edith Abrahams. *Integrating Arts and Crafts in the Jewish School: A Step-by-Step Guide, Vol. I: Kindergarten to Second Grade*. New York: Behrman House, Inc., 1979.

Teaching arts and crafts is really simple when you use this book as a guide. Just as the title promises, Tauben and Abrahams take you step-by-step through every small detail. Everything is already worked out for the Jewish school up through grade two—even to the approximate amount and kind of supplies that should be ordered in advance. Most notably, the book includes key cognitive questions which enhance and clarify the purpose of the projects for the students. Even if you are teaching arts and crafts to older students, you will want to see how the authors do this.

Thomas, Murray R., and Sherwin G. Swartout. *Integrated Teaching Materials*, rev. ed. New York: McKay, 1963.

Check this book out if you are looking for a wide variety of activities and techniques to be used in teaching the social studies aspects of your curriculum.

Wallen, Carl J., and LaDonna L. Wallen. *Effective Classroom Management*. Boston: Allyn and Bacon, Inc., 1978.

Because this is the third team of married educators cited in this list, I want to digress to point out what a wonderful profession teaching can be for those who share it with the ones they love. So much for that. This is a down-to-earth, everything-you-need-to-know, how-and-why-to-do-it book. You will appreciate it from the moment you open it until the last page has been read. You will thank me for pointing it out to you. I use it all the time to refresh my memory of what classroom management can be.

Whitehead, Alfred N.. *Adventures of Ideas*. New York: The Macmillan Company, 1933.
——*Modes of Thought*. New York: The Macmillan Company, 1938.
——*Religion in the Making*. New York: The Macmillan Company, 1926.
——*The Aims of Education*. New York: The Macmillan Company, 1929.

The fact is that I have been influenced as much by Whitehead as by Dewey, Buber, and Highet. He is the master theoretician of education. He did not merely found a school, as Dewey did; or expound a philosophy, as Buber did; or represent fine teaching, as Highet did—Whitehead encompassed them all. It is strange that I did not quote Whitehead or cite his thinking specifically in the writing of this particular book. I will rectify that. It is fitting and appropriate to close with a quote from *The Aims of Education*, wherein Whitehead wrote, "An easy book ought to be burned for it cannot be educational."

For the sake of my teachers, I hope that you have found my book straightforward and practical, but not necessarily "easy" in all its parts. What Whitehead says about books can also be extrapolated to apply to the task of teaching itself, to wit: Those who believe that teaching is easy should not bother teaching, for what they are teaching can hardly be worth learning.